FINDING WHAT'S
MISSING

www.mascotbooks.com

Finding What's Missing

I have tried to recreate events, locales, and conversations from my memories of them. In order to maintain their anonymity, in some instances I have changed the names of individuals and places. I may have changed some identifying characteristics and details such as physical properties, occupations, and places of residence.

The views and opinions expressed in this book are solely those of the author. These views and opinions do not necessarily represent those of the publisher or staff.

Although the author and publisher have made every effort to ensure that the information in this book was correct at press time, the author and publisher do not assume and hereby disclaim any liability to any party for any loss, damage, or disruption caused by errors or omissions, whether such errors or omissions result from negligence, accident, or any other cause.

For more information, please contact:
Mascot Books
620 Herndon Parkway #320
Herndon, VA 20170
info@mascotbooks.com

Library of Congress Control Number: 2020920948

CPSIA Code: PRV1220A
ISBN-13: 978-1-64543-134-3

Printed in the United States

This book is dedicated to my husband, Anthony, the one person in my life who loves me for who I truly am...not the wounded, broken child I had been. He has helped me grow into the kind of person he knew I could be. Thank you, Anthony, for believing in me when I didn't even believe in myself.

FINDING WHAT'S *Missing*

JoAnn Manali

My story contains depictions of emotional, verbal, sexual, and physical abuse. Reader discretion is advised.

CONTENTS

REASONS FOR WRITING MY STORY

I wrote this because I wanted to help children who are in the same situation I came from. I wanted to give them hope and the expectation they could overcome extremely difficult times. The real message of this story is, "How did she do that?" Children don't see the end of difficulty; they just see the difficult times. They need a sense of completion and finality to combat the idea that the difficulty will last forever.

It doesn't. I hope that the children who are trying to find their way will believe in themselves. They must be dreamers, and then they must realize they can achieve their dreams and find a way out through persistence. I hope this story shows them that they can succeed.

Another reason I'm writing this story is because of Anthony, my husband and the first person to love me unconditionally. He helped me heal from my past and learn to love– something I didn't know how to do. I thank him and hope the story helps his family understand me better, so we can all be better people. I want to thank Anthony for introducing me to Peter White, a wonderful man, husband, and international social worker. If I hadn't met Peter and learned what an outstanding person he was, I would never have written this book. He helped me understand that, "In helping others, we help ourselves." Giving back is very good therapy for me. Thank you, Peter.

When I began writing this book, life was a lot more difficult than it currently is. Anthony stood with me through those extremely difficult times, and our love grew stronger. He's my superhero. Thank you, my love!

I also wrote this in honor of my sister who passed away. I can't believe I survived this story when my brother and sister didn't, and my other siblings became ruined from it. They live in another world.

1

I was born in Buffalo, New York, on August 4, 1964, making me a Leo, which means I was meant to be a strong person and a leader. I would need all that birth-given strength and more. I was one of eight children, born in the middle of four boys and four girls, making me the third-youngest girl.

We were very poor. Macaroni and cheese from a box was gourmet dining for us when we could get it. Usually, we had bread and flour gravy, made without sausage. Tomato and mayo sandwiches were also quite popular, although sometimes we didn't have tomatoes. As an adult, I always refuse gravy or tomatoes.

Mom was a good cook when she made meals. Our stepfather often ate steak and potatoes. When times were good, she made spaghetti and meatballs, which were delicious. Those times were when her family visited and our cousins stayed for dinner, and played with us. Those memorable family gatherings soon stopped.

Mom wasn't a very loving mother the way most mothers are. She didn't give hugs or kisses and never said, "I love you."

She'd been married three times. Her first husband, Jack Woodson, gave her three children: Tom, Jen, and John. When things didn't work out, they divorced.

Then she met my father, Carmine, and had four more children: Marcie, me (JoAnn), Maria, and Carmine Jr. That didn't last long either, and they divorced.

The stories Mom told about Jack were fairly mild, but those about Carmine were horrendous. South Buffalo was, and still is, a rough place. We moved within the area many times. As I recall, we moved so much because Mom couldn't afford the rent and we would get kicked out. We mostly stayed in South Buffalo and we did get to know the neighborhoods well. I observed that different ethnic groups tended to group together in different regions of the city: the Irish lived in South Buffalo, the Polish gathered in North Buffalo, the West Side was mostly Italian, and the East Side was where colored folk built their community.

My first memories were that I never talked. I didn't even say "goo-goo" or "ga-ga" until the age of five. I had to take speech classes until I was ten to learn how to speak properly. Apparently, the abuse was so bad, I never spoke a word.

We didn't get proper food so we were all very skinny, and we never had any attention, love, or guidance. We lived in a constant state of nerves, fearing we'd upset our parents and be beaten. They made us kneel on floor grates, eat soap, and starve in our rooms with the windows nailed shut. All I learned from them was alcohol and more alcohol. All they did was drink every day, all day and night. That is all I ever saw them do, and that led them to abuse me and the other kids. Then came more abuse, as they didn't love or even like us.

That was evident to me at a very young age. My earliest memories have no hugging, kissing, or attention of any kind. We were in the way, and we knew it. Jen, my half-sister, took care of us and became our parent. She knew how to communicate with me and gave me food and water when I pointed.

Food was a big deal. We weren't allowed to touch anything in the kitchen. We never knew what was in the fridge, and we knew if we touched anything in there, we'd be grounded and beaten with a belt. I didn't open a refrigerator until I was fifteen. I was amazed at what I saw.

One evening when I was eight, I awoke in the middle of the night and was famished. I decided to sneak downstairs and look in the cupboard–another thing we weren't allowed to touch, but maybe I'd find something to eat.

I found peanut butter and was shocked when I saw it. Then I found bread and had a few bites, but accidentally made some noise. I had awoken Mom, who slept nearby, and she was furious. She didn't care when I told her how hungry I was. She took my sandwich and beat me down the hall until I ran upstairs to cry myself to sleep again.

I was angry when I realized that they had peanut butter but we weren't allowed to have any. It was torture to go to bed hungry after being beaten. We were constantly stressed. All I wanted was to be loved. Was that asking too much?

They made me feel worse than a dog. We had dogs, and they were treated better than we were. As an adult, when I see a child being loved and realize I never experienced anything like that while growing up, I think, *Why couldn't that have been me? Why me? What did I do?*

It's a daily struggle not to think about my past and how I survived when I see normal kids being loved and having vacations, all while I struggled to get food and water.

Carmine abused Jen the way he abused all of us. He was evil, and he looked it. We were terrified of him. He broke Mom's nose five times during their short marriage–once by shoving her through plate glass. Tom and Jen were sexually assaulted and beaten many times. John had a permanent fat lip as a result of being punched constantly. Carmine shoved Mom down a flight of stairs while she was pregnant with Carmine Jr., and he was messed up for life.

Because I never talked, my parents thought I was mentally challenged. I pointed a lot. If I wanted water, I pointed at the bathroom faucet. Once, when Carmine wanted me to say "water" and I refused, he punched me, chipping my teeth with the ring on his finger. I flew from the door into the tub, tearing open my chin and eye. I needed stitches.

I was too scared to speak. I knew something terrible happened because my nightmares continued into adulthood. I still scare easily and scream when frightened. It's not a regular scream–I *scream.* I also wake up at night to find myself crying in my sleep.

None of us kids got through life without a broken nose, dislocated jaw, and numerous scars. Once, when Carmine's mother visited us, I had a friction burn on my face.

"What happened to you?" she asked.

"She spilled cereal from her high chair onto the floor,"

Carmine lied. "Her mother rubbed her face into the carpet and the mess."

He was Satan incarnated, and his mother knew it too. She created a devil, and it was passed on to his children. He finally died of colon cancer at the age of fifty-nine. I hoped he rotted in hell.

Finally, Mom called the cops and had Carmine put in jail. She sold his motorcycle and divorced him. It wasn't easy to get rid of him. He was psychotic and enjoyed torturing us. Sometimes while Mom was at a local pub, which she did a lot, Carmine came home to scare us. He wore masks to terrify us.

He set our apartment–which was above a pizzeria–on fire when I was four. Firefighters had to rescue me from my bed. Half of it was on fire when someone wrapped a blanket around me to get me out. Asphyxiated by the smoke, I fell into a deeper sleep. Because I wouldn't talk, the firemen weren't sure if I was okay, but they finally let me run to my aunt's house a few doors down, wearing only my tee shirt and underwear. To this day, I'm terrified of fire.

Finally, Mom met Brad Harlan at the local bar, and she married him. They had a son named Cole. Carmine still came around to frighten us when he could, but that slowed and eventually stopped.

At first, Brad was good to us kids, especially while he dated Mom. He bought bikes for the older boys. He was so nice to us, and eventually I began talking.

"Wow. She never talked before," my siblings said.

Doctors said I was too abused to talk, but with five years of speech classes, I would be fine. When I grew up, people said I wouldn't shut up.

I refuse to have children because of my abusive childhood.

I am too frightened of passing that behavior on. I would never let any child endure such a thing.

Once Cole was born, the situation began to change, which our Christmas pictures showed. Finally, we had none of those pictures. My entire life with seven siblings was documented only by enough photos to fill a single shoebox. We did not have photo albums like regular folks did. I saw one of me at around thirteen years old and that was the last picture I've seen of myself from that time period. Although Brad was abusive to the rest of us, he never did anything to Cole. He was never grounded, slapped, or starved like we were. We knew he was spoiled.

We had chores to do, were grounded frequently for nothing, beaten with belts, and sent back to the end of the line to start over again. We were forced to kneel on the heating grates in the floor, and sometimes forced to hold books for hours.

As well as not knowing what was in the refrigerator, we had to set down our forks when we ate. After every bite of food off the fork, we would have to place the fork down and chew our food. Only after the bite was fully chewed and swallowed could we pick the fork back up to get the next bite of food and do it over and over again. He said we ate too fast and that this would stop that. I say we were starving and did eat faster than most kids. We enjoyed the free summer lunches at Cazenovia Park because they put something between the slices of bread in their sandwiches. We stood in line for free blocks of cheese, though none of us were allowed to eat it.

We went to bed hungry almost every night. Tom sold chocolate bars for the Boy Scouts. He was allowed to join the Boy Scouts, even though no one else could. John was nicknamed

"Klepto," short for kleptomaniac, because he stole Tom's candy, and we were grounded for it. Jen even got out the Bible, and we swore on it that we didn't steal the candy. Even John swore, even though he was the thief.

For fun, when we were old enough, we shoveled snow just to get out of the house. We made a lot of money doing that, because there were five of us old enough to work. We gave Mom the money, and she sometimes gave us a dollar. We were happy about that until we didn't get anything at all. It snowed a lot in Buffalo, so people always needed their driveways cleared.

In the summer, we were always on our own. Mom made us get out of the house once our chores were done. We stayed outside all day until lunch, then dinner, then bedtime, when we heard the infamous whistle. We knew if we didn't come running at that sound, we'd be in trouble.

We played many times in the YMCA parking lot. I never went inside the Y. I taught Maria to ride her bike, which was supposed to be mine. Marcie told me what I got for Christmas one year, and Brad found out. He gave it to Maria instead and made me teach her to ride it. I didn't know how to ride, so I first had to learn, then I had to teach her. I felt when Brad saw us kids, he saw our fathers and didn't like us for that. It seemed to get worse as we grew older.

At school, I saw a lot of differences in the other kids. They could talk when they wanted, they had nice clothes and shoes, and they had lunch money. They could speak in front of the class about their summer vacations. I heard about all the good times the other kids had. Whenever the teacher called on me to tell my vacation story, I never had one.

To this day, when I see TV commercials about Disney

World and kids going on vacation with their families, I can never imagine it for myself. Just thinking about it gives me gooseflesh. Why did they get to go? I didn't see Disney World until I was thirty.

Attending speech classes brought a lot of bullying. I tried to win Mom's love by being a good student at school. I was a straight-A student, on the honor roll, and won the spelling bee. I was in constant competition with my oldest brother, someone I looked up to. He was also very smart in school.

The other kids didn't seem to enjoy school as much as Tom and I. Jen went just to get out of the house. None of us missed a day, although John skipped often and tried to teach us how. We attended Public School No. 28, a half-mile walk past two school guards–three if we went to the candy store before school.

I was eight years old, and we could never afford anything, let alone candy. One day, John gave me a buck for my gloves at school for a snowball fight. Not all of us had gloves–only the younger kids had them–and they were too big for my hands, so I gave him the gloves and went to the candy store.

Halfway there, I saw an older man leaning against a white, four-door car, smiling at me. I naively smiled back and kept my eyes on my route. At the corner of the candy store, I saw a cop talking with the crossing guard. I bought some candy, and the crossing guard walked me across the street back toward school.

The man with the white car stood there with the passenger door open, and he was still smiling. When I ignored him, he grabbed me from behind. I wore ugly red boots I slipped over my shoes and a white zippered jacket. He lifted me up, smiling and laughing, and turned me around while I kept running in place. Terrified, I couldn't believe he was trying to kidnap me.

I unzipped my jacket and slipped my arms out as I ran to the policeman and crossing guard.

The guard didn't know me well, because I usually couldn't afford candy, and he didn't believe my story even though all I wore was a sweater. She and the cop had a boy walk me to school to the crossing guard who knew me better.

She didn't have a radio to call the police, so she had the boy walk me to the next guard closer to my house, who had a radio. By that time, I was freezing.

When the police arrived, they questioned me like an adult, asking what make and model car it was and if I remembered the license plate. Terrified, all I could say was that it was white with four doors. They were very intimidating and didn't believe me, so they sent me home alone without a jacket. They didn't even offer me a ride.

When I walked to school, there were always older kids around. I passed a small park on the way home that we usually cut through, but it looked too creepy that day so I stayed on the sidewalk near the street. Then, up came the pervert in his car with the passenger window down. He almost stopped on Talbot Road, the main street, smiling and waving with his nasty smile to show me he'd been following me the whole time.

It wasn't much farther to home, so I ran as fast as I could. I was sure he was following me. We lived on a corner of Talbot Road.

I went in through the back door where Mom sat at the kitchen table reading her morning newspaper while Gram had coffee. She lived upstairs with Aunt Jackie. Brad was away at work.

Mom saw me coming through a side window. She sat

around the house all day, watching soap operas while she had us do all the chores, from mopping to dusting.

I was too out of breath to talk, and she kept asking where my jacket was. When I finally told her and Gram what happened, Mom was furious that the cops sent me home alone without my jacket. I felt good to know that she and Gram felt bad for me, and I was home safe with them. I never saw that pervert again.

I knew Mom did not love me when I was little. How could she not? When she allowed us to do dishonest things, she taught us wrong, but we were too young to know better. Brad and Mom even took us to cornfields to steal corn. No one ever showed me how to get it. They just took us out there at night. We all, as kids, had to work hard to fill Brad's trunk.

The first time, I pulled the whole stalk from the ground, thinking it was hard work. I came back with the stalk and the others laughed, then someone showed me how to break off the ears.

When I was ten, Jerry Lewis was a big deal. We collected money for his charity. Watching for our names on his show was a lot of fun. We decorated our old coffee cans and taped crayon pictures to the cans. We cut slits into the top and went to the supermarket to ask for donations for Jerry. Because we were poor, many people thought it was cute. Feeling sorry for us, they gave us money. We were six kids with cans of change; the money added up fast.

When watching Jerry Lewis on TV, we looked for the Harlan Clan–named after Brad–hoping to hear our name, but it never happened. Mom and Brad kept all the money and sent us back out for more. We never knew about it for years, as we looked forward to the telethon, while Mom and Dad looked forward to it even more. We looked forward to it because we got out of the house and away from our mean parents.

Mom had twelve brothers and sisters. In the early years, they were close. Uncle Harry, her oldest brother, and Uncle Barry, her younger brother, were good to us. Uncle Harry had six kids. On Sundays, Mom made sauce and we got together for the day, alternating visiting either house. Those were fun times with my cousins. It was too bad there were so few.

Aunt Sara, who had one son, was also close to Mom. He was very spoiled and had all the toys we'd ever heard of. I used him to get candy and toys we didn't have. I loved little Davey, but I never saw him after Aunt Sara died of lung cancer at age thirty-two. We were on the verge of leaving Buffalo at the time and didn't attend the funeral; nor did my mother or stepfather. Aunt Sara chose the dress she wanted to wear in her casket, chose the casket, took family portraits, and peacefully passed away. She knew we had a rough life, and she was good to us kids.

Aunt Karen was pretty nice too. She lived in West Seneca, a suburb of Buffalo, with a better way of life. She and Uncle Doug had two kids and a huge yard with a ravine. In the summer, we hiked the ravine and wooded area. In the winter, we went sledding in her backyard with tin garbage can lids. We hung onto the sides and put our whole bodies on the lids. That was a blast. I will always remember the easy way of having good fun without money, just using our good sense.

Our next great snow adventure was a park with a real toboggan. That was great fun. We waxed the steel blades, then went down a chute before racing down the hill. Four or five of us got on the toboggan. We went a long way with that much weight. That was probably the most memorable fun I had as a kid. We had to work as a team, and it took all of us. We had no idea at the time that such fun was hard to come by.

Aunt Jackie was the wild child among Mom's sisters. To this day, she will always remind me of Maria. She wore mini-skirts. Wow, they were short! I never saw a woman like Aunt Jackie before. She always arrived on a Harley Davidson motorcycle with whatever guy she was dating that week.

On the way to school was a candy store we never got to visit. One day, Aunt Jackie came out of a local bar across the street and saw us walking to school. She knew we never had candy or treats. She let us have a heyday in the store. We loved her and never told on her. She did that for us many times during our school years. Aunt Jackie lived upstairs with Gram, where her biker friends came to get her frequently. I often wondered if she wore panties with her tall black boots and short skirts.

I wasn't the only one who wondered. Tom and John found a way to get up the staircase and looked in Aunt Jackie's closet. They told stories of going up when they were alone in the house, and they sometimes said they saw Aunt Jackie changing clothes.

Grandpa passed away in Florida, which was why Aunt Jackie and Gram lived together. Grandpa retired to Fort Pierce, Florida, on the East Coast. Like most Yankees, he shuttled between the two areas until he died of a heart attack at the age of sixty-two. From Mom's stories, he was very strict, which she passed on to us. I always had fond memories of Grandpa and felt he regretted treating his children the way he did once he got to know us as innocent kids. He tried to spoil us because we'd never known such treatment. He passed down bad ways to the next generation, which continued the tradition. He bought us candy and let us sit on his lap. Sometimes, he let us ride in his Cadillac. I was glad we had some nice treatment from someone. We loved Gramps, or at least I did. We didn't have love at home and didn't know how to receive it.

The first time I received a real hug, I didn't know what it meant. My fourth grade teacher's last name was hard to spell. Between my maiden last name and hers, I learned to spell well. I practiced for the school spelling bees that were held once a year in the auditorium. It was fun, pretty nerve-wracking, and challenging. One year, I won first place. My teacher had a party with a cake and decorations.

I was upset. I wanted to go home and tell Mom I won, and that I didn't just take second or third place. It didn't matter if I won or even if I entered. She wouldn't have loved me under any circumstances. Still, I thought that if I won, she would love me.

My teacher knew me better than I understood. She kept trying to calm me down, but I was stubborn and didn't want to have fun with the other kids. I sat in the back of the class being stubborn, and she came up to give me a bear hug. I squirmed and tried to get away, but she didn't let go. She held me and said, "Stay still, child. I'm trying to give you a hug."

Finally, I stopped resisting, and it felt good. I was nine years old, and I didn't know what a hug was. That was my first hug. I wondered why I didn't get those at home.

That was when I knew I wasn't like the other kids at school. I never went to their houses or used the telephone. I didn't know what a sleepover was. Kids talked about summer vacations, but I never had one and assumed they were for rich people. Mom never hugged us or anyone else. Relatives came to visit and gave us little hugs, but it didn't mean much. They were just saying hello before we were sent out to play.

Our relatives felt sorry for us and often got into fights with

Mom and Dad over the way they treated us. That made them angry, so they treated us worse.

One house catty-corner from ours had an Italian family. The smells that came from that house were wonderful. One day, I couldn't resist and went over. The woman gave me food that seemed unreal. I didn't remember what it was, but it smelled and tasted divine. The visit was burned into my memory. They didn't know me, but they were good to me anyway. Back at home, I was beaten with a belt and told never to visit anyone's house. After that, I never did. The neighbors knew how strictly we were being raised.

Being the way he was, Brad once told me, "You can't move until you learn to tie your shoes."

He didn't bother showing me how.

I sat there until I figured out a way to tie my shoes. It wasn't the way other people did it, but it worked for me and still does. One time, Maria's son was grounded for the same thing. I stopped to show him my way of tying shoes, and he learned how to do it.

My fondest memories all come from our younger years. As time passed, life grew worse. Mom had trouble dealing with all of us, especially when we called her Mom. She said not to say that. We had to do all the chores–dishes, vacuuming, dusting, mopping, clothes washing . . . We called her Mom because we wanted her love and attention, but instead she had a nervous breakdown.

We were good kids. We didn't run around all the time or refuse to listen. Our relatives agreed we were well-behaved. We knew we'd be beaten for anything we did wrong.

I was often called a boy because Mom gave me haircuts

herself, and I looked like a boy. Sometimes, when I did the dishes, family or a rare visitor would say, "What a nice boy." Boys never did dishes around the house.

Around that time, Mom found out that Brad was abusing Marcie in the basement when Mom wasn't around. After she found out, Mom went on strike. She put a big sign in the window that read "Strike" when she found out about Marcie and Brad. TV crews arrived and put the sign on TV. Suddenly, half the neighborhood moms were on strike. Mom started a trend.

Unfortunately, Mom began having mental trouble. The doctor gave her Valium. Brad's torture grew worse. Eating became almost impossible. He had us set down our forks each time we brought it close to our mouths, then we had to set our hands in our laps. He made Cole and me do that every meal. He said we ate too fast, so he wanted to make us chew our food more.

We never had snacks like juice, fruit, or even water, so we were starving by mealtime. I'm sure I ate quickly.

One evening we had beef stew, which was another great meal Mom eventually stopped making. I was very sick, but no one would let me stay in bed. I kept telling them I was sick, but to no avail except threats of punishment.

I threw up on my plate because I wasn't allowed to leave the table. They took me to the bathroom and made me take a bite from a bar of soap, then they beat my ass and sent me to my room for punishment. There was no talk of medicine. No one cared that I was so sick that I threw up.

After seeing me throw up, they made all the kids eat all the food on their plates. Brad was upset because I ruined his dinner, and he didn't eat any more after seeing me be sick.

Being grounded in my room was normal. I thought all kids were grounded, but I was wrong. Sometimes other kids came to our front yard and called up to us, but we were grounded and couldn't come out. They threw candy to the roof and we crawled out the window to get it because getting candy was so rare. Brad caught us and nailed the windows shut. It was very hot in the summer with the windows closed, but no one cared. We never had central air-conditioning.

We were so bored, we counted the cars passing by on the street. We played games while grounded to pass the time, but if we heard footsteps coming up the stairs, we shook with fear, knowing a beating was coming. Once, I was so hungry that I ate my blanket, gnawing on it until only half was left. I was beaten for that and grounded for even longer.

Days turned into months. We couldn't wait for school so we could get out of the house and get good lunches. The beatings were getting worse, too. The older we got, the harder the beatings were. If we were really bad, they turned the belt around and used the buckle end against our bare butts. Begging for them to stop just enraged them, and they kept beating, wanting us to shut up, but we were crying from the pain. They didn't care.

The pain was unbearable. They sent the ones who cried to the back of the line so we'd be beaten a second time. Sometimes, we'd be sent to the back of the line three times. We had bruises everywhere, but no one helped us.

We did have some neighbors Mom and Brad got along with. They got them to join the Moose Club, and they drank there a lot. Once, we went on a Moose picnic. It was unbelievable to see so many kids. We played hide-and-seek, and there was an old refrigerator on the property, which I hid in. I locked myself in accidentally and ended up beating on the door to get out until a kid finally heard me and opened it, saving my life.

As a family we took minimal photographs. The Christmas ones seemed normal, but they weren't. Mom and Dad drank constantly. They stayed out late at bars and came home early in the morning. Finally, they allowed Tom to feed us while they slept, because we knocked on the bedroom door to say we were hungry and wanted breakfast. They were enraged at being woken up. We prayed they wouldn't beat our asses for doing that, so we sent Cole, knowing they didn't beat him. They sometimes slept until the afternoon.

We starved until Tom was finally allowed to feed us. We ate puffed wheat cereal in a bowl with powdered milk. That was awful, but we were so hungry, we ate it and liked it. Tom started feeling proud of being the leader.

Around the age of ten, anything I thought of as normal changed. The last Christmas when I got any presents, I received a Crissy doll that had hair that could grow. I loved that doll.

After that year, we were given onions and charcoal and were told we'd been bad and didn't deserve presents–except for Cole. He got nice toys. Once Brad knew how to torment us, he did it constantly. Every day, our lives grew worse, except for Marcie's.

She seemed able to do the same things we did without being grounded or beaten. She stomped her feet going up the stairs, and we were the ones dragged down by our hair to go back up without making a sound. I was too young to figure out that Marcie was doing bad things with Brad in the basement. They went down there a lot, and I didn't learn about it until years later, when she told me about it. She also told me Brad turned Tom and John into devils. He blindfolded her and made her suck their penises, saying it was a lollypop. It was no wonder she had nightmares of being raped and beaten and still needs drugs to cope even today.

The whole time Brad was around, I felt he was trying to break our spirits. I refused. I kept praying to God to help us. I wasn't even sure God existed, but still I prayed. I wanted to be adopted and taken out of that hell. I was a tomboy who liked sports and hated dresses, but Brad made me wear one every day to school. They were gifts from our cousins to Mom. If there was anything he could do to make me angry or hurt, he did it and laughed.

Tom also babysat when Mom and Brad went to the bars. He was worse than they were at times, locking us in closets or making us kneel on grates. The evil ways were being passed down. Brad flicked our ears or grabbed them to steer us where he wanted us to go. Now, I've seen Cole do that to his stepchildren, although he never does that to his own kids.

Mom's family continued arguing. Brad created plenty of friction with her brothers and sisters. He was too mean to us, and they'd seen us kneeling, starving, and crying. Anyone who stuck up for us was told not to come back.

Kids made fun of me at school because I wore dresses, while they had cool clothes like jeans and regular shirts. All our clothes were hand-me-downs from Goodwill. We didn't know how to act when we first visited a mall or clothing store. I was an adult of thirty before I understood how to act in those situations. I went on TV for the Jerry Lewis telethon for special needs children, making them braces and artificial legs. I went to the mall to buy something to wear for the TV show and suddenly started crying to the saleswoman, trying to explain what I needed.

Sometimes our cousins gave us cool clothes, which we got to wear. I once wore jeans to school. Brad was working the graveyard shift and didn't see what we wore. I was in line with my class, as we went upstairs, and a girl grabbed the back of my jeans and tugged on them. They were four times my size, but I wanted to wear them so badly. I fought with some of the kids who laughed at me. It was traumatizing to have them do such things to me, but it was nothing compared to my life at home. Soon, Brad lost his job at the Bethlehem Steel Company working on the railroad. He and Mom got into an argument, and he never tried to go back to work there.

Concerning Mom taking Valium and having a breakdown, I thought she caught Brad and Marcie in the basement. I was just a kid, but I knew something was going on. At least her breakdown didn't last long.

2

W e moved to Cleveland, Ohio, when I was ten and in the fifth grade. It was an industrial city, which explained why we moved there: so that Brad could get a job.

Back in Buffalo, our biological father married and impregnated Mom's sister, Aunt Jackie. She looked a lot like Mom, and Aunt Jackie told Mom that sometimes Carmine called her Mom's name in the bedroom. Eventually, she left him and the child.

Did that mean my aunt was my stepmom? Was their child my cousin or my sister? It was a mess. I never met the girl.

Brad found a job, and we enrolled in new schools. Cleveland was a tougher city than Buffalo. We lived on the west side at Lorraine and 105th. I went to St. Ignatius Church on Sundays.

I loved church. I didn't hear a lot, but I certainly prayed to

God a lot. Going to church got us out of the house.

I wasn't sure there was a God. Recently, someone asked if I told my story when I attended Bible lessons.

"No," I replied. "Looking back, if we went to Bible classes, we would have learned what they did to us was wrong, and we'd tell somebody."

In Cleveland, the boys began stealing bicycles from grocery stores, churches, and other locations. They swapped the parts and resold them. I didn't know about it until John used me as a pawn by pushing me into some kids while he took off on someone's bike. When I went home, I saw John and Tom with Brad and realized what they were doing. Brad was teaching them bad ways.

Uncle Pat moved to Cleveland and lived next door. He looked and acted like John, my brother, and they were the same: devious, conniving, lying, and willing to cut someone's throat. Uncle Pat brought Aunt Sharon, his wife, and their two kids. They stayed for two years.

Tom and John, as the two eldest, received the worst torture of all of us. Jen had epileptic seizures and fell down shaking–something very traumatic to witness. Our parents accused her of doing it on purpose and grounded her or beat her. They called her an actress. They never took her to a doctor.

I asked if she remembered her convulsions, but she didn't, although she had clear memories of the beatings.

She came into the bedroom, acting distraught and saying, "This isn't natural." The rest of us didn't know what she meant. She tried to run away, but Tom found her and took her home. She begged him not to, but he said if he didn't, Brad would have his way with him. I remembered the speech Brad gave

Tom before he left. He warned Tom not to come back without Jen. She cried constantly when she was brought back, and they beat her until she bled.

Tom, who was seventeen, asked if he could join the army early. He wanted to leave home because he didn't want to see us younger kids being beaten. Brad said it was okay. They signed papers to let Tom leave school early to join the army. He became an army surveyor. I always looked up to him and would miss him.

John continued stealing things. At night, Jen told us we were being abused, and other kids didn't live like we did. We began to believe her. Marcie continued to get away with things, but I saw that Mom disliked Marcie more as time passed. Mom and Brad fought about Marcie often.

Jen was only fifteen, and she wanted out badly. One night, as Brad nailed the windows shut again so that she couldn't escape, he said, "Pack your bags and get out now!"

We heard everything in the next room, and Jen came in to pack. Most kids would have cried, but not Jen. She was happy. She promised she'd see us again someday, but it was many years before we did.

Jen's departure impacted all of us, but it was especially hard on Maria. After Jen left, Mom and Brad wouldn't say anything about why she was gone. If we mentioned Jen's name, they immediately said negative things about her, adding that it was good she was gone.

I kept remembering the happy expression on Jen's face when she left. I understood it more and more as time passed. She was tortured for a long time, as I was. Maria never forgave Jen for not returning to help us as she promised. I was terrified, as I awaited my turn someday.

We never told our teachers what was going on at home because we were too terrified of our parents. There was no one I could trust. Tom was in the army, and Jen left. I was sure Marcie was still having sex with Brad or at least doing sexual things with him. She started that behavior when she was twelve. She was ahead of the rest of us and talked about sex as a kid. Brad didn't help matters.

I saw more tension growing between Mom and Marcie. Brad feared Jen would return and tell someone what he was doing, so we moved to make it impossible for her to find us.

We moved to Phoenix, Arizona. Mom and Brad declared there was no way Jen would ever find us. I called it abandonment.

We helped Mom pack for the move. Brad returned from the school with our transcripts when an awful scream came from the basement.

Marcie caught her hand in the washing machine while it was spinning, trying to slow it down. John and I ran downstairs and unplugged the machine, stopping it. Her arm was broken in four places.

After seeing a doctor, Marcie was in a lot of pain, moaning and groaning, as we drove across America. I wished Mom would have given her the pills to quiet her, but she only gave her a little bit and not at the right times–only when she was tired of hearing Marcie cry. It was a long, hard drive for all of us.

We arrived and found a house, then we got placed in a school. I loved living in Arizona. The school was cool. We walked outside from building to building. We had lots of breaks, and little stores on campus sold drinks and snacks. I was amazed. Kids played Frisbee during breaks. I learned quickly and became good at it.

I got along well with my classmates. A really cute boy in my class became my friend. I was very naïve. He was my first kiss. I dreamed about that kiss for a long time. I never kissed a boy before and never asked anyone how to do it. He certainly knew how, and I followed along. It felt good to have someone like me.

I took a photography class and loved it. We were in a valley with mountains all around, which was quite a change from the cities we knew.

I was grounded when we left Cleveland, and I stayed grounded in Arizona until summer ended. I hated Brad, and the feeling was mutual. I took as many classes at school as I could, no matter where we lived.

Brad couldn't find a job in Phoenix, and he and Mom drank away all their money. Brad always got large checks from the IRS each year because he claimed all eight of us as deductions, whether we lived at home or not.

When another of those checks arrived, we had enough money to move to Riverview, Florida. Brad knew someone there, and we moved in with them. They were very nice people.

We soon moved down the street to our own single-wide trailer, but we had to clear the land first. We used sickles to cut down the overgrown bushes, plants, and brush on the property that were too large for a lawnmower to cut down. That was tough work.

There was a small pond in the backyard with a little dock we could fish from. That pond gave me many happy memories, learning to fish and setting trout lines with John. He was good with nature and could live off the land. Later, that was what he did.

We placed chicken guts into pantyhose with a knot tied

on each end to prevent the guts from spilling out. We added a hook to the pantyhose and used it to catch snapping turtles. They were really good food. John taught me how to clean and cook them. They were delicious. At first, I didn't want to eat them, but I was so hungry that I tried it. I learned to like them cooked in flour and then fried.

John also had a little boat with a rod and reel for fishing. I had a cane pole. He showed me how to make bread balls as bait for wild shiners, which I gave to John to use as bait for largemouth bass.

I fell in love with fishing and almost lived on that dock. It took me away from all the problems at home. Fishing became therapy for me. No one was yelling or screaming at me, or telling me I was wrong. I wasn't constantly nervous while on the dock. It was just silence until I caught a fish; then I was excited and wondered what I had on the end of my line.

I never stopped fishing. Eventually I bought a dingy, then a bass boat, then I moved on to an eighteen-foot Ranger saltwater boat, a twenty-two-foot Ranger bay boat, a thirty-two-foot MAKO offshore boat, a thirty-four-foot Hydra-Sports boat, and finally a thirty-six-foot Yellowfin.

The Davies who lived next door to us and had a daughter were nice Southern people. Each lot was one or two acres, so they weren't actually that close, but close enough to see what was going on.

Mr. Davies quickly came to dislike Brad's ways. He was loud, obnoxious, and didn't respect anyone. All of us, including Mom, were too skinny, except for Marcie and Brad.

Mom and Brad allowed me to babysit for Mrs. Davies' daughter. That was my first job, though of course Mom and

Brad took all the money. The Davies cared for me. They treated me differently than how I was treated at home, and I didn't want to leave their house, but I knew better than to say anything. They felt awful for us kids and disliked Mom and Brad more each day.

Brad wanted to terrorize Mr. Davies, so he bought a bull. Mr. Davies thought it was awful for the poor animal. The first bull we had was named Yankee, and the second was Supper. That made Mr. Davies angry, but Brad found it funny. Brad was mean to everyone and got a kick out of it.

I met Trisha, a girl my age who lived across the street on a few acres and owned a horse. She was nice enough to allow John and me on her property, and she taught us how to ride horses. She was very patient while teaching us. Eventually, we could ride bareback.

One day, Brad bought a horse. The seller knew that Brad knew nothing about horses because we came from New York, so he drugged an ornery horse to make it calm and sold it to Brad. When Trisha came over to give the horse a test ride, she did great. She ran that horse all over, with and without a saddle.

A day later, the horse went wild, chasing and biting us. One day after school, John and I went out to ride the horse. The moment we came near it to put it on the tack, the horse chased us. Faster than we were, she came at us like a bull. John shoved me forward, helping me run faster to get away. The horse bit John before we escaped, taking a chunk out of his shoulder.

We tried to break the horse with Trisha's help, but we finally had a vet come out, who told us the horse wasn't old enough to ride. It was only a year and a half old, and horses shouldn't be ridden until they are two. We wound up with a horse we couldn't ride.

Through Trisha, I met a lady who had horses that needed to be ridden. I promised to feed and wash the animals and to walk them after riding–anything I could do for them. The lady agreed. She was single, and the three horses weren't getting the attention they needed. The horses had been spoiled by barn life. They didn't want to ride away from the property, so it was difficult getting them to leave. On the way home, I had to hang on because they galloped back toward the barn, sometimes swiping against a tree to knock me off. That was why the lady wanted me to work her horses. They forgot their discipline if they weren't ridden regularly.

They needed bathing and brushing, and I was in heaven working with them. We had a lot in common. Working with the horses was soothing. I came to love those horses and took good care of them. When Trisha and I went riding, it was so much fun, especially when Mom wanted me out of the house all day.

Other than fishing and riding, summers were long and hot. I loved fishing and the chance to get away from my parents and all our problems. Sometimes, if we had enough kids for a team, we played softball in the yard.

We couldn't swim in the pond because it had rattlesnakes, water moccasins, and alligators. We had to be very careful when fishing around the pond. The dock boards had separated with age, and a water moccasin came up between them near my feet. I ran to John, who kept a shovel nearby for killing snakes, and he got rid of it.

Uncle Pat and Aunt Sharon moved near us, bringing their two little kids. It was nice to have them visit. We never went anywhere or did anything. One year, McDonald's had a contest to see if anyone could say, "two all-beef patties, special sauce, lettuce, cheese, pickles, onions on a sesame seed bun" in ten seconds. Anyone who could do it got the food for free. That was my first Big Mac.

Mom's sisters from Buffalo came to visit, and got drunk and rode the bull, Yankee. He didn't like it and went near the pond, where he bucked Aunt Hariet off. She flew over the bull's head and went into the water, laughing all the way. I was worried, knowing about the snakes and alligators in the pond, but they kept riding the bull. It was hilarious.

While they visited, we went to Coquina Beach, by Bradenton Beach. I was amazed at seeing picnic tables and grills where people had cookouts. We loved playing in the ocean and the sand. We had to watch each other and come back before lunch or dinner. Those were good times at the beach.

After Mom's sisters returned home, they never visited again, but we went to the beach a few times. Mom loved it. Her brother lived across the state in Fort Lauderdale, and we visited him a few times. He lived near a beach on the Atlantic Ocean. I never saw waves that big before. I didn't know how to swim, so I was careful not to go in over my head. The undertow and riptides were dangerous, and they caught me many times. I was lucky to get free of them. When I tumbled underwater, I did my best to swim away. I almost drowned more than once. Brad rented boogie boards and then kept them. They helped keep us afloat.

Before we left, Mom and her brother got into a fight about the way Brad treated us, as well as how rude he was. After that, we never saw him again, nor did we return to the beach.

School was great. Getting out of the house and into air-conditioning was nice. I loved to learn, and getting fed was a bonus. John and Marcie were in the school next to mine, where I would go the following year. That was hard on me, because they quickly got bad reputations.

Marcie did some crazy stuff and started hanging out with colored boys, which was unusual in those days. She sneaked out at night to meet them.

One day, they took some of Brad's guns to school. He left them out around the house. John also stole Brad's fireworks, like M-80s. He flushed them down the toilet at school to blow up the pipes. Because of John's shenanigans, the doors to the stalls were taken off.

According to John, they took two loaded pistols to school to shoot some black kids who were mad at Marcie. As they were eating in the cafeteria, police surrounded the building. Marcie saw them and ditched her gun in the school's garbage can. The police saw her do it and quickly arrested her, putting her in handcuffs. They pulled the gun out of the trash as evidence.

John, seeing Marcie, panicked, and shoved the gun against the dean's back and told everyone not to move. The dean, a woman, eventually talked him into putting down the gun and surrendering to the police, promising not to press charges, but it took hours to convince him.

After John and Marcie were taken to the police station, they were released without any formal charges being filed. Both were immediately expelled from school. The dean had always liked John, although I never understood why. Maybe she felt sorry for him. She was a big lesbian who looked like John Wayne.

Once at school, John took too many pills. The dean called me to her office to ask my opinion of John, but when I walked in, I found John robbing her desk, handing me things he took. He couldn't talk. His tongue was so thick, I couldn't understand a word. I tried to tell him to put everything back, and then I walked out of the office. The dean expected me to stick up for him, but I refused.

Instead, I told them to call an ambulance and to call Mom. I had to sit in the waiting area for them. When Mom and Brad arrived, they were furious because I was chewing gum. They would be even angrier when they saw John.

They went into the office, and I heard John being slapped several times. I doubted he even felt it. The ambulance arrived, and Mom took John to the hospital to have his stomach pumped, which saved his life. He overdosed on Valium. I never knew where he got them. He said later that they were expired, so he didn't think they were still strong.

I came home from school one day to find Marcie gone without any explanation. Later, John disappeared the same way. We weren't allowed to ask about them or say their names. It was like they never existed.

I was next in line, and I felt pressure building on me. There was a pattern to it–the three oldest kids leaving home–which made me wonder if I would be the next one to be abandoned. I was only thirteen and didn't know how to prepare for something like that.

One day, Brad touched my breast, and I ran away from him. I was terrified he would get me at night, so I hardly slept. We were always crammed into beds with one or two other kids. Even as an adult, sleeping on a California king-sized bed, I cling to the edge of the mattress.

I was forced to sleep on the couch where Brad watched TV.

I wasn't able to sleep much, because I was too worried.

Food grew less and less as our money dwindled. As before, we ate tomato and Miracle Whip sandwiches, sometimes without the tomatoes.

A tragic event happened before John left. Mom told us to go to the store, which meant a one-mile walk each way through the woods. We walked everywhere, which gave me awesome calf muscles, so that was no problem.

On the way, John said he had to pee, so I waited by the road. He came out of the woods a minute later, and we went on our way. When we walked back toward home, we found the woods on fire. John smiled at the scene, and I knew he started it. I was glad when someone called the fire department, and they put out the fire, although it almost completely cleared the woods and reached nearby trailers where people lived.

Soon after that, John disappeared.

3

We packed up and moved back to Cleveland, but into a rougher area than where we lived before. Mom and Brad said they didn't want Marcie finding us. A relative of Liza Minnelli lived next door. She might have been Liza's sister. Liza visited her, and there were many photographs of the two of them around the house. Liza was nice to us, too.

School was very rough. There were gangs with guns, kids with pipes, and plenty of fights. Once again, we were summoned to stick up for each other no matter what, or we'd face serious punishment at home. It was so bad, we actually helped each other.

Those two years in Cleveland challenged me mentally, because the torture increased. Jen came home one day. I was in the driveway with the other kids, and Jen walked up to us with a big smile. I didn't recognize her immediately.

"Is that you, Jen?" I asked.

"Yes." She hugged me.

She was beautiful. She wore normal clothes and makeup and looked good.

"I want to see Mom," Jen said.

I ran into the house and told Mom that Jen was outside. Mom immediately called all of us kids into the house, then she called the cops.

When the police came, Mom demanded that Jen get off her property. The police made her leave. I didn't understand why Jen didn't explain the reason she left the family. Maybe she didn't want to return. Maria and I were disappointed that Jen didn't help us younger children, even though she knew what we endured each day. Mom and Brad talked about Jen constantly, saying we had to hate her, she was a bad person, and we shouldn't consider her family. It was crazy how much they hated her. They took their madness out on us, and since I was the oldest, I got most of that.

I began watching *Saturday Night Live* and *Don Kirshner's Rock Concert* on Saturday nights because John watched those shows. I inherited John's TV when he left and we moved back to Cleveland. I loved those programs.

Brad knew that, and it struck him as the perfect time to torture me. He and Mom were pretty drunk or high at that time of night, so they called me into the living room to tell me how awful Jen was. Marcie didn't get that treatment as much as I did. They sometimes sat me down at the dining room table for hours to hammer at me with their terrible thoughts. It was awful, but I never let them know it bothered me. That apparently bothered them more.

"I love my family, all of them," I kept saying.

It was sometimes three or four o'clock in the morning before they stopped harassing me and let me go to bed.

Tom came home on leave from the army to visit. It didn't take Brad long to react. I loved Tom and looked up to him. He and I were the smartest kids in the family. It drove Brad crazy to see me excited about seeing Tom. He was so angry with me, he slapped me hard enough to knock me off the chair.

Tom was angry, which was part of Brad's plan. "Did you have to hit her so hard?"

"What are you going to do about it, boy?"

Tom had no chance in a fight with Brad, and both knew it.

"You can leave now. We can do whatever we want to these kids, and there isn't a damn thing you can do about it."

Tom left, and it was many years before I saw him again.

I felt disappointed when Tom didn't try to get the cops to help us. My nights of torture grew worse and became much longer. They harped on Jen and Tom, trying to get me to say I hated Tom, Jen, John, and Marcie. They made me say out loud that I hated them. Anyone who left home was no good.

I stopped watching TV and pretended to sleep in an effort to avoid the abuse. It didn't help much because I was terrified about what might happen if they saw I wasn't really sleeping. They'd take me downstairs to torture me again, making me sit and listen to their antics. Brad convinced Mom to follow his lead in everything. She never once tried to stop him. When Brad wasn't home, and we begged for food and water, she threatened us and said she'd tell on us, which made us shake.

John returned home one evening all bloody, like he was dying. He apparently had been stabbed again, or so he said. He had to hold his stomach with his hands to keep his guts inside. Brad rushed him to a nearby hospital, where they stitched him up and placed a colostomy outside his stomach. After he healed, they planned to put it back where it belonged. He had an incision from the top of his chest to his belly button, as if he had a heart attack and needed surgery.

"They asked me if I wanted my belly button," John told me, "and I said yes."

"What about the first stabbing?" I asked.

"Marcie and I got into it with some guys, and they stabbed me. I almost bled to death. She called an ambulance to help me. There was another time when I was taking a stereo out of a car, and a guy caught me and tried to cut my throat. I shoved my hand up just in time and got my hand cut open."

I loved John, but I knew I couldn't trust him.

He lived with us while he healed, with part of his internal organs in a bag outside his stomach. Brad faked punching him in the stomach, making him cringe, and Brad laughed. It was heartbreaking to see what he did to John. At least some of the torture was taken away from me.

It took John a long time to heal. He stole Mom's liquor and beer and hid it in the snow outside the back door. Once he was well enough, John got a job at a gas station pumping gas. The owner eventually gave him the keys to the place, which was a bad idea.

One night, John summoned me down from my room to help unload things into the basement. I carried cases of beer and Coke, bags filled with cigarette cartons, and other bags full of candy and chips. It looked like he emptied the store.

Brad, John, and Uncle Pat robbed the place and broke some of the glass to make it look like a break-in. They were never caught.

Soon afterward, we moved to Phoenix, Arizona. John had no trouble leaving. He had already hitchhiked across the country with Tom, or by himself. When John healed enough and had enough of Brad, he disappeared again. I never knew how he found us in Cleveland. Out of all the kids, John was allowed to return home for a while. I knew Tom, Jen, and Marcie would never come home, nor would I, Maria, or Carmine Jr.–just John.

We moved back to Florida. I was fourteen and knew my time at home was almost over. We moved and settled into school, and I loved it as usual because I could get away from Mom and Brad. I couldn't wait for my turn to escape.

I met a lot of good kids. I didn't have any reputation problems despite being related to John and Marcie. People didn't know what to think of me. I was a good kid, and the teachers and the dean knew it. I wasn't perfect, but no kid was. Since I wanted to be there, I never skipped school. I had to become somebody, which meant staying in school.

We were so screwed up as kids, we never thought of going to college. All we worried about was how we would eat and what clothes and shoes we could wear. Mom always kept the clothes from the older kids, so we wore them when we were bigger. I never went to a mall, Walmart, or any store other than a 7-Eleven where Mom sent us to buy things.

None of us knew how to act in a restaurant, a store, a movie theater, or anywhere public, because we never got to go. We were just slaves.

The torture from Brad continued, and I was near my breaking point. He knew it too. I prayed to God each day, asking Him to protect me and begging I would be adopted. Mom was just as bad as Brad, calling me terrible names, yet I was always a good kid.

One evening, after more taunting, I overheard them talking together about how to get rid of me. They discussed scaring me to make me run like Jen did. They took me from my room to torture me some more.

Their attitude was so bad, they finally called the police to take me away. The officers said there was nothing they could do, because I wasn't a runaway and hadn't committed a crime. Mom and Brad were furious.

"We want her out of this house," Brad said. "Take her to a home or someplace."

"No," the officer said. "She hasn't done anything."

Finally, after a lot of persistence, the police took me someplace that would scare me. It worked, even though I knew I hadn't done anything. It was like a jail. My parents tried to abandon me at a place that held delinquent and wayward children.

Once we were there, the police started asking me questions. I answered politely, something bad kids with bad attitudes never did. I tried to tell them my parents were bad people and I wasn't. I shyly pleaded with them to believe me.

They took me out right away before I was escorted to part of the home where the abuse happened. Once we were back at the reception area, I was surprised my parents were still there. They hadn't abandoned me after all.

The beatings and mental torture continued. I went blank. They knew I wasn't listening anymore, especially when I didn't hear their questions, which made them even more angry.

They sabotaged my bedroom in hope of finding something, but they never did. They removed the door to make sure I wasn't doing anything wrong in my room.

4

When I was fifteen, my day finally came. They told me to take a few things and get out, and I didn't hesitate. First, they had me say goodbye to my younger siblings, which was something they hadn't done with the other kids. Saying goodbye to the three who were still home, I wondered if I'd ever see them again. I was anxious to leave.

I knew a girl from school named Donna who lived down the road. I'd seen the bus drop her off in front of her house. I never visited anyone's house before, nor called anyone on the phone. I walked the mile to her house and told her what happened, asking if I could stay awhile. She agreed.

That was my first time in a friend's house, and I didn't know how to act or what to do. I cried. My friend and her mom were gracious to me. I went to school as if nothing happened and didn't tell anyone for a while.

When I finally told some other friends, they said their parents agreed to let me live at their houses as long as I was in school. They were better equipped to take care of me than Donna's mom. It sounded great, so I went.

I started seeing things I'd never seen before like food, telephones, new clothes, and TV anytime someone wanted to watch. It was unbelievable. I saw people give each other love and hugs. Those moments became embedded in my mind.

Apparently some of the kids at school began talking about me, saying it wasn't normal for me to live with another family. The word eventually got back to the principal.

One day, I was getting ready for school when the police arrived and told me I had to come with them. I freaked out and started crying, begging them to let me stay. When the mother insisted I had to leave with the police, I was terrified.

"Where are you taking me?" I asked.

"You're going back to New York where your parents are. They'll pick you up at the airport."

Crying, I said, "They won't be there. I'm sure of it. You're sending me somewhere I know nobody. We've been away a long time."

"Your parents will be there."

"I'm the fifth kid they've thrown out of the house. I assure you they won't be at the airport. Mom abandoned all of us."

They pretended not to hear me. It was clear they didn't care.

I had a police escort onto the plane before anyone else boarded. They also gave me a large envelope and told me not to open it before I reached New York. When other passengers boarded the plane, they looked at me like I was a criminal, fearing I must have done something terrible and might do it to them too. It was horrible.

That was my first flight on a plane. It was unbelievable to see such a huge machine rise into the air and descend with ease. The clouds were like pillows.

When I arrived at the Buffalo airport, I waited in my seat for an officer to come get me. As the passengers filed out of the plane, they looked at me judgingly. Once everyone was off the plane, I left. No one I knew was in sight. All the other passengers were greeted by someone, but not me. I'd never been in an airport alone before, and it was as big as a city.

Alone and hungry, I roamed the halls, wandering aimlessly. Finally, not knowing what to do and hoping someone might be looking for me, I went to a lady and asked her to page someone looking for JoAnn to meet her at gate six. No one came, of course. I asked her to do that twice more before I gave up.

I noticed a police station attached to the airport and walked there to turn myself in with the envelope I wasn't allowed to open. The Florida authorities must have known my parents weren't in New York, but they flew me there because it was my birthplace. Hungry and upset, I went to the police station and saw a man sitting behind his desk.

I walked up to him and threw the envelope down on the desk. "Now just open the damn thing. They told me not to open it, but you go ahead."

The shocked officer didn't know what to do. It was raining hard outside.

"I'm starving," I said.

He took me to a halfway house, something I'd never heard of before. It wasn't pretty. There were people of all ages except mine, waiting between jail and their home life. I was scared to death someone would attack me in the night. It was very hard to go to sleep.

I woke in the morning to see the older people eating. I was starving, and they gave me breakfast. They were actually nice to me. When I told my story, they couldn't believe it.

I stayed there for several days before the state of New York figured out what to do with me. They put me in a temporary foster home. It was a very nice place with other girls who were also waiting to be fostered. I didn't know anything about foster homes and what they were about. The owners were Italian. The father didn't speak English. They taught us good things to know, like how to wash and iron clothes. We had to iron our clothes every day. I learned how to make a bed properly and to eat properly. The wife taught me how to cook, which was something Mom never showed any of us.

They were very loving and took a liking to me. I liked them too, maybe because I was Italian. They showed me how to use a knife, and not just a butter knife. They were patient people who listened to our stories.

They had an older child in college, and they really missed her and thought I might fill in for her. The mother swore she was psychic, which scared me. I'd been through enough already. She told me about my aunt who had passed away, and she read my palm, saying I had a short lifespan with a broken lifeline on my hand, which was scary.

They liked me and wanted me to stay because I was Italian, but I declined. I was ready to live on my own. I'd done all that praying to find someone to adopt me, and there I was, thinking I was tough enough to live on my own.

I was sent to my aunt's house, Mom's youngest sister, who lived in Blasdell, a suburb of Buffalo. Her family welcomed me and were good to me. I went to school and enjoyed it, and I did well. I seemed happy. My aunt and uncle had two kids, plus one from a previous marriage.

On the outside, they seemed great, but they fought a lot. Billy, a kid at school, befriended me. I was totally naïve about having friends or boyfriends, so I trusted that he liked me. I was smart and figured he needed help. I let him cheat from my papers at school and tried to teach him.

He asked me to come over to his house one day, and that soon became a recurring event. I didn't usually enter someone's home without knocking, but I was at Billy's house so often, he told me to just walk in. Most days, we went through schoolwork or had a snack.

That went on for a while until I got to know his mom, brothers, and dog. His dad was never around. No one asked me too much, and I was polite.

One day, I went to Billy's house and walked in through the back door into the kitchen with its table and chairs. A large, dark-haired man with shoulder-length hair sat at the end of the table alone.

He looked at me. In that moment, where I thought I'd never know my real father even if he walked by me on the street, I stared and asked, "Are you JoAnn?"

"Yes."

I almost fell over from shock and anger. He sat there with his leg shaking, as if he were nervous.

"Won't you sit down so we can talk things over?" he asked.

I believed in God and wanted to forgive him, but as I

sat down, I felt even angrier. "Why? Why'd you abuse my sister, Jen?"

"It wasn't me. It was my brother. He looks just like me."

"Okay. What about my brother? You kicked my mom down the stairs when she was pregnant."

"Look, the past is in the past. Can't we go forward?"

I thought he was sincere. He said he had a family and lived in Detroit, Michigan.

"I'd love to get to know you," he said. "How about coming to Detroit and giving me a chance to know you?"

Then his girlfriend and Billy walked into the kitchen. I didn't know he was married or that he was there with his girlfriend. He was there cheating on his wife with Billy's mom; I should have known he was bad news from the start. It finally sank in that Billy befriended me for all the wrong reasons, and that hurt.

I ran home to find Aunt D and Uncle Rick fighting again. I felt out of place there. They couldn't afford a teenager, even though I didn't ask for much. I was always polite and grateful to those who housed and fed me.

I decided to accept Carmine's offer and go to Michigan. Aunt D and Uncle Rick weren't happy about it, but there was nothing they could do. My mind was made up.

It was a long drive to Detroit, but we arrived safely. That was the first time I broke the law, because I left New York without permission. I met Carmine's wife and new baby. They were nice to me for a while.

I enrolled in the local school, but it was still summertime. Carmine was a truck driver who liked to race his car. He did well at racing. He made it to the Indianapolis Grand National

Race, which meant he had to qualify at different national races first. It was awesome–a great time in my life. The big dogs of racing were there, and I got to meet them and get their auto-graphed photos.

It was a five-day race. Carmine lasted for three days. We had pit passes the whole time. While at the track, the car was taped off so no one could touch it, but we still had to watch in case someone walked by to toss a bolt or nut into the engine. Carmine warned me that other people would be willing to sab-otage their opponents.

In my free time, I wandered through the pits, collecting signatures and meeting other drivers. When I got bored, I went into the stands and sat down to get a view. It was a lot of fun. I met some people who were also watching.

We stayed at a campsite for trailers and RVs near the track, where electricity was available. Carmine had a trailer to haul his car and other equipment.

On the third day, Carmine spun out, which eliminated him from the race. The third night, he let me sit in the passenger side of the racecar, which had no seat, and we went out for a drive. It was so fast, it seemed unreal!

After we returned home from the races, Carmine had to go to work. He asked me to accompany him to the state of Washington and down through California to drop off a load in Nevada, then return to Michigan. We seemed to get along, and he said it would be a great way to get to know each other, so I agreed. I would be the navigator. Carmine said he wasn't that good with maps.

It was a very long trip. We stopped at truck stops to eat and clean up. Those were pretty rough places. Carmine ate, then he smoked pot and took speed he bought from dealers at the stops. I also learned his truck was overweight.

He wanted to bypass the weigh stations, so we mapped out a route through the mountains that took us past them. Even though he took speed, he fell asleep while driving through the mountains. Once, I saw us getting close to the guard rail and looked over to find him asleep. I freaked out, thinking I would die going over a cliff, so I slapped his arm.

"We're going over the side!" I shouted.

He turned the wheel just in time to avoid breaking through the guard rail. After that, I never slept while he drove because I didn't trust him. I was very lucky I'd been awake at that time. I fed him candy and suckers to help keep him awake. When he smoked a joint, it acted like speed on him.

One day in Oregon, we drove down the road and he kept staring at me. We were in a big truck and if we crashed, it wouldn't be pretty. He needed to pay attention to the road.

"What are you looking at?" I asked.

"You look just like your mother, the fucking cunt."

I still hated Mom, but nobody said things like that about her.

"Fuck you, asshole."

He immediately pulled over on the side of the road, reached over the hump in the middle of the cab, and pulled my arm behind my back.

"What did you say?" he demanded.

"Fuck you! You heard me!"

He dislocated my shoulder, then he punched me hard enough to dislocate my jaw. He punched the other side of my face to put my jaw back. I thought I was going to die.

Since he couldn't fix my shoulder, he had to take me to a hospital. He made me say I fell out of the truck and hurt my arm. I was too scared to disobey, so I didn't say anything when the doctors fixed me up. He promised to kill me if I didn't lie.

I just wanted to get back to Detroit and never go on a road trip with him again.

When we finally got home, the beatings started. I never knew when or where, and it wasn't just me. He beat his wife too. She picked up the baby for protection, but that didn't help. He still beat her and called her terrible names.

He worked on his racecar in the garage. When he started the engine, he always got lots of attention. All the boys came around to see the car. The lady across the street called the cops to complain about the noise and all the people. I made friends with her.

Carmine did the craziest things, like wake me from sleeping by squirting ketchup or mustard all over my face. It was awful. He threw his coffee cup or the drink in his hand at me. I thought he got past his anger issues, but they were getting worse.

When I went to school, I started meeting new people, which was nice. At night, sometimes kids from school walked by the house and hollered for me to come out. I would be on the couch and would look out the window. If I asked for permission to go out, Carmine always said no. I finally stopped asking and quit looking out the window.

Even hearing my friends outside made him angry. He came over to grab me and threw me down, kicking me with his boots. I tried to protect myself as best I could. Sometimes, he hit my head hard enough to knock me out.

One day, I fell asleep in the backyard where there were a table and some chairs. They were turned upside down to keep rain off them, but I set down two chairs, one for me and another for my feet, then I fell asleep.

When I woke up, I heard him screaming, "Where is she?" I jumped up without putting the chairs back and ran into him at the side of the house. He was furious. He threw his cup of hot coffee at me, then grabbed me. I tried to explain that I was sleeping in the backyard.

A nineteen-year-old boy next door came out. He was a big kid, and he said, "Stop hitting her."

"I'll do the same thing to you," Carmine warned.

The kid went back into his house.

Carmine threw me into the bushes, then pulled me back out and dragged me to the front yard. He got on top of me and choked me until I passed out.

I awoke in the yard later that night. I couldn't believe the lady across the street who called the cops all the time didn't bother for that one, nor had the boy next door. The first thing I did was touch my neck, expecting blood, but my hands came back clean.

I crawled up the stairs into the house and went into the bathroom. Freaking out, I started crying because I didn't recognize myself. My neck had huge bruises. I saw his handprints all around my neck. It almost looked like he tried to strangle me twice. My nose was broken, and my eyes were black and covered in dried blood. I was a mess. My ribs hurt from where he apparently kicked me on the ground.

I had to get away from the mirror. I went into the living room and sat on a corner of the couch to regroup, shaking and scared to death, when I heard the front door open and Carmine walked in.

"I'll bet you never do that again. If you call the police, I'll hunt you down and kill you."

He didn't offer to take me to the hospital.

When I was younger, he went to prison many times. His family disowned him, thinking he was crazy. He did many terrible things to us when we were kids. Once, I heard the ice cream truck coming and I wanted ice cream. Carmine bought me a cone and sat me on his knee until I asked for it, but I wasn't talking at the time. Finally, he let me go, but without the ice cream.

I couldn't leave the house until my bruises healed. The kids at school asked what happened. Word got around pretty fast, but no one did anything to help. The kids suggested I leave.

There were no more road trips after the first one. I'd been with Carmine only six months.

One day when I was doing dishes in the kitchen, he came up behind me and groped my breasts. He was a big man, and I was much smaller. When I turned around, he had a gun in his hand, which he put against my head.

"What are you going to do?" he asked.

I planned to fight for my life, but just then, the front door opened. His boss stood in the doorway with a clear view of the kitchen.

"What are you doing?" he demanded.

Carmine put the gun away, and I ran to my bedroom and shut the door. Shivering in bed, I knew I had to leave. If I stayed, I would die. I didn't dare sleep at all.

Monday, on the way to school, I called the New York State Office of Children and Family Services. I didn't have any money, but I convinced the operator that the call was important, so she put it through. When they answered, I told the person my name and where I was. I explained what happened already and what I feared was coming.

"If you don't help me," I said, "I'll kill myself. I can't take any more. I'm willing to go anywhere you put me if you can please get me out of here right away."

"Go to the airport. A ticket will be waiting for you."

That made me happy, but I still had to get to the airport. I told some kids at school I trusted, and they said they'd help. I had to go home and pack some clothes, then they'd take me to the airport.

When I got home later that day, I tried to act normal, but I was terrified. Everyone finally went to sleep. My clothes were in the back room, where the baby slept across from Carmine's room.

I took careful, terrifying steps down that hall to reach the room, knowing Carmine kept a gun under his pillow and woke easily due to his time in prison. I packed my small amount of clothes in a bag and crept back down the hall. Once I was sure Carmine was still asleep, I took my bag to an alley I passed on my way to school, hid it in the bushes, then I went back to the house to wait for morning.

Eventually, dawn came. I hadn't slept all night. Acting as normally as I could, I went to school. When my friends picked me up, it was the happiest day of my life. We got my bag, and I cried at the thought that I might die. They consoled me and took me to my flight.

I never wanted to see Carmine again, and I didn't. He died at the age of fifty-nine from colon cancer. I hoped it was painful.

5

When I arrived in New York, I was sixteen. The authorities didn't know what to do with me. Since I left the state without notifying them, I had broken the law, so I ended up in a group home with thirty other girls. They weren't very nice. All were bad enough to have done something to be placed there. It was in Buffalo's West Side, a rough part of the city although I couldn't leave to find out. Only the girls with parents could be picked up for events on weekends. I did not have parents to pick me up, so I had to stay there. At least the other kids got out. I had nowhere to go and was stuck there 24/7.

The girls were mean, and I got into plenty of fights. I was often punished with kitchen duty for more than thirty people, but I was just defending myself. At least I got good at that.

Finally, I was tired of it all and asked to go before a judge.

Some of the girls were good at fighting but didn't want to better themselves, but I did.

I went before the same lady judge in family court. While in the group home, I met a girl who was my stepfather's sister's daughter. She said I could live with her.

The judge agreed and allowed me to transfer, giving my step-aunt money to help care for me, plus monthly allowances for a growing girl's needs. I was happy to leave the group home and thought the new situation would be better.

My step-aunt lived in South Buffalo where I was born. When I got to South Buffalo, six girls jumped me and beat the crap out of me just for being the new girl in town. All I could do to protect myself was to curl into a ball. Later, I tracked down all six of them one at a time and returned the favor, beating them as hard as they beat me. Life in South Buffalo was tough with plenty of fighting.

Late one night, I was on a corner with another girl, and a boy came out of a bar and punched me without warning, knocking me out. I had a black eye the next morning.

I went to his house and knocked, hoping to find out what was going on. His mother answered the door.

"This is what your son did to me," I said. "He was on LSD last night."

She called the father to the door, but he didn't believe me. I hoped he would punish the boy, but it never happened.

I told Linda, a friend of mine, about it. She later joined the Marine Corps. She told me not to worry. We waited one evening in an alley near the boy's house. When he came walking home, Linda jumped out with a baseball bat and hit his knees. He fell down in pain, badly injured.

"You keep your hands off her," Linda said, walking away. There goes your baseball career," she added, knowing he was very athletic.

He never bothered me again.

I started dating an Italian boy named Tony. A girl named Peggy who didn't like me used to date Tony, and she wanted him back. We ran in the same circles, because I was athletic too. I hung out with jocks and other kids. Usually, I got along with everyone. When I saw Peggy, I walked the other way because she was very big and intimidating.

One evening, I saw her at a local bar where I played pool, so I left. I ran into some friends hanging out at the corner near the local bar. A friend just bought a fifteen-speed, all aluminum bike. I never owned a bike and asked if I could take a spin on it. I was in awe of that bike. It was so smooth and lightweight.

Peggy saw me and came out with a friend who was even bigger than she was. They started talking nasty in front of my friends on the corner. It was embarrassing, but I acted like I didn't hear. She threw a cocktail glass at me in the middle of the road, and it broke the spokes on my friend's new bike. She was upset and told me to fight Peggy.

In New York, fights on the street were common. People always crowded around like watching a boxing match. Peggy scared me with her talk of kicking the crap out of me, and all the others egged me on.

I agreed with the condition that we got off the main road and used a side street where the cops wouldn't see us. She took off her sweater and was getting ready to fight, talking nasty all the way. She removed her wooden clogs, then put them back on to follow me.

My friend with the bike talked to me like a boxing coach, giving me lots of tips. All I asked for was a fair fight and not to let her friend jump me, and they agreed.

The fight began. It wasn't pretty. All I could think of was my sister, Marcie. She was a big girl. If she got hold of someone, she won. I had to come out strong and not let Peggy get on top of me.

As we fought, I knocked her head against a car bumper, hoping to stun her. It worked. She fell down. Knowing what she would have done to me, I took one of her clogs and used the heel to smash in her face, telling her, "This is what you were going to do to me!"

The fight was over. When her friend jumped me, my friends pulled her off. She went to help Peggy. Someone called 911 for an ambulance because Peggy was bleeding too much.

The police came to see what was going on. Mr. Manny, who owned the pizza shop across the street, saw it all and said I was just defending myself after Peggy threw a glass at me and then attacked me. I bought pizza from Mr. Manny all the time, and he always remembered Italians.

No charges were filed. Peggy never bothered me again.

I stayed in the same room as my cousin, who was two years younger. She had two brothers. One was two years younger than her, the other was five years older. Both were still at home. They were very strange boys. I could tell something wasn't right with them.

Soon, my few clothes disappeared. No one knew where they went, and Aunt D locked her bedroom when she wasn't around, as did Berry, her son. Bobbie, the youngest, broke into her room to get things of his she'd locked up. One day, I looked in while he was breaking in and saw all my clothes with the tags still on them. Furious, I took them to my room, only to find them missing again the next morning.

Aunt D was evil, just like her brother, Brad. She looked like him too. She gave me a curfew of eight o'clock, but often I was with her kids. If I was locked out, so were they. If I wasn't with them, then I was locked out for the night. They never gave me a key. Many nights, I slept in the small area between the front door and the porch door in an attempt to protect myself from the Lake Erie winds, which created record-breaking low temperatures. I begged, cried, and pleaded with them to let me in, but they refused. If they answered, they said I missed curfew, so it was too bad.

I was forced to pee in my pants and was cold and hungry. Once again, I begged God, if He existed, to help me. What had I done to deserve such things?

One night, I woke up on the pull-out couch to find Berry on the couch, too, feeling me. I freaked out, and he ran away in the dark to his room like the snake he was. I was ready the next time. I knew no one would believe me if I told them. I had to wound him so it would show on the outside.

I waited, and he eventually came out, sneaking through the bottom of my covers. He reached my calf when I kicked his face as hard as I could. I continued kicking him with both feet. He ran down the hall as fast as he could. I screamed at him, calling him a pervert, but no one came out to help. The others pretended they were sleeping.

The next morning, Berry was injured, as I had hoped. I told the rest of the family about what he did and added, "I'm going to talk to the judge."

I left to find a friend's house where I could stay. I told her mom how I was being locked out and about weird Berry. I asked to appear before a judge again, and I got the same lady judge as before.

I spent all night rehearsing what I wanted to say. I wrote it all down and memorized it.

When the time came, I did great. I used many words above my age level. As I hoped, I impressed her.

"What do you want?" she asked me.

"I want to finish high school and go to college. I want to be on my own, to become somebody. I'm the best one who knows how to take care of me. I've never gotten into trouble other, than leaving New York. I deserve a chance."

Looking at my grades, she noticed I also had a job after school. "Yes," she said. "I will monitor you through the Independent Living Program. You'll have to report to me occasionally, so you'd better do well in school."

I kept up my end of the deal, reporting to her as instructed. Due to all the traveling my parents did, I had a lot of school credits. By my senior year, I had more than necessary, so I had to attend school only half a day for half the year. I graduated early and got the judge's approval to start college early.

When I appeared before her, she said something I will always remember. "You have been an exemplary example for the state of New York. You can stay, and New York will pay for you until you're twenty-one years old."

I felt highly honored.

"This doesn't happen often enough," she added.

I lived with my friend and paid her mom rent. My friend went into the military, while I started college.

I missed fishing during that time. Soon, it seemed everyone was in a rut. My friends both joined the service, but no one else had any aspirations. They would stay where they were forever.

I spent eighteen months attending community college, taking a city bus to and from both college and work. My boyfriend cheated on me. Ironically enough, it was with a girl from Florida.

I reached out to my oldest brother, asking if I could stay with him awhile, and he agreed. I arranged to take a Greyhound bus from Buffalo to Clearwater, Florida. When I went to say goodbye to my friends, they didn't believe I was really leaving.

I had enough of that city, its people, and the weather. I wanted out of there and felt very disappointed.

I arrived in Florida at the age of nineteen after a long, scary bus ride. I was back where the fishing and sun were, but I was very lonely and missed Tony most of all. I called him and cried over the phone, saying how much I missed him. It became embarrassing, so I quit calling.

I moved from Tom's house in Clearwater to Marcie's house in Tampa. I wasn't sure which was worse. I didn't stay in Clearwater for long, because Tom's duplex caught fire, killing his next-door neighbor. I hadn't even been there long enough to get a job. Now no one had a place to live, so Tom went to his mother-in-law's and I found Marcie's house. Once I left New York, I also lost the paychecks I was receiving, so I had to find a better-paying job. Marcie was always a worker. She didn't sit around and watch soap operas all day. She had a construction job doing glass work on high-rises in downtown Tampa, so she got me a job with her. I was good with my hands and learned quickly.

I really needed a job and did the things other people were afraid to do to ensure I'd stay employed. One day, a twenty-two-story building needed glass installed from the outside. The workers would need a swing stage that hung from the top of the building. The problem was that the building wasn't flush all the way. It had an angle from which the operator would have to swing the stage eighteen stories up until the inside crew could tie off the ropes. Then they would hand out huge sheets of glass from the inside of the building to be installed on the outside.

We had to do an eighteen-story double skylight, and I did that job with my boss. We got out on the swing stage and tied our safety ropes in case of failure. Someone handed us sheets of glass from the inside. When the boss stepped onto the stage, it moved up five feet, scaring me half to death. I controlled a motor to level us out.

The situation at Marcie's got so bad, I needed out. Her neighbor was a good person who said I could stay there. Marcie was still hanging out with guys who were very abusive. When they thought they could abuse me, though, they were wrong. I never understood why Marcie let herself be punched in the face and why she took all the abuse from them.

The only problem with moving next door was there was only one bedroom, but I didn't care. I was willing to do anything to get out of Marcie's. I slept on the couch. I came home so tired, I sometimes fell asleep on the couch before I showered, only to get up the next day in the same clothes to catch the city bus from North Tampa into downtown, an hour-and-a-half drive. When I carried tools and was dirt poor, people on the bus stared at me.

I saw plenty of mishaps on the job. Once, a claw hammer

fell seventeen stories. The hammer barely missed a guy and stuck in the truck bed beside him.

Another time, a guy was on a ladder doing electrical work when his ladder kicked out from under him. He was left up at the ceiling, hanging from the wires. My boss walked around the corner and saw what happened. A big man, he managed to pull the guy off. He walked off the job and quit that day, he was so scared.

Another day, we were drilling concrete to set the frame for holding the glass. It was a long day. We worked on a two-story scaffold, predrilling the building for the metal work. I hung off the second story of the scaffold. We were working at the twentieth floor.

Near the end of the day, I was pushing the drill too hard when the bit finally went through the concrete. I almost fell off with the sudden change. I was tied off as usual, but if I'd gone out of the building, the scaffold would have come with me. I really had to calm down after that one.

I realized I couldn't do manual labor my entire life. I had to find another career. I talked with the crane operators, saying they needed more women on the job. They tried to discourage me with magazine articles about potential accidents.

There were two cage-like elevators on the outside of the building to take you up to your floor for the day, called buck hoists. One day, trying to impress and prove to the crane operators that I could do the job, I jumped into a steel box that was supposed to be used for tools only. When I jumped in, I said, "Floor eighteen is where I'm working today. Take me up." The crane operator took me up past all the people in the buck hoists and delivered me to my floor, and I went to work.

The next day when I arrived at work, everyone was outside waiting for me to get there for a general contractors meeting. The general contractor wanted me fired for getting in that box. A different set of people had recently done the same thing as I had, but the box fell and killed everyone in it. OSHA (the Occupational Safety and Health Administration) refused to let anyone else ride in the boxes. My boss refused to let the general contractor fire me, and said he needed me because no one else was willing to do the things I did. I got to keep my job.

When the job ended, I was recommended to the fifth-largest glass company in the country. I learned a lot about residential glass work, opposed to the commercial that I'd done earlier. It was good learning how to cut glass and install it, then how to cut and install mirrors.

One day, the foreman and I were disposing of defective glass in a dumpster out back. The corner struck a piece of metal and broke. The glass sheet was so large it took two of us to lift. Glass makes a terrible noise right before it breaks–a noise I got used to hearing. I heard the glass sheet I was carrying creak with strain, so I turned my head away just in time before it shattered in front of me. My hands were still in place, and the glass cut my left wrist severely. Blood spurted everywhere from the artery.

At the hospital, the doctor stitched my wrist back together, but I'd lost some nerves too. My hand felt numb, and I dropped things without thinking. If someone stuck me with a pin, I didn't flinch. It took years for those nerves to regrow.

Soon I got back to work, supposedly doing lighter duty work, like sweeping. Instead they had me at the H. Lee Moffitt Cancer Center installing half-inch X-ray glass. It would take five pieces of glass per frame so the radiation didn't effect anyone. I was in a sink installing these by myself and had all five pieces in when I reached for my drill to place the framing to hold the glass together, and my hand went numb, losing grip on the glass. The first piece hit me on the head, then went over my head and knocked me out of the sink on top of the glass. Four more pieces of glass came down on top of me and knocked me out. When I came to, there was an electrician there who heard all the noise and came to see what had happened. I was covered in blood and looked pretty bad, but after getting stitched up, it really could have been much worse, so I was grateful.

I knew it was time to move on from glass. I had various jobs. I learned to tend bar, which was fun, but I wanted more from life. I met a boy and shared an apartment with him. We both worked to make ends meet. We got along for a few years–going to bars, playing pool, darts, foosball, and hanging out. Eventually, that got old, and I needed more.

My sister offered to have me come to Tennessee and stay with her for a while. I was twenty-one by then, and my boyfriend cheated on me, so I was ready to leave. I needed money to get there, so I sold my old, beat-up car and paid someone to drive me to Tennessee, where Jen picked me up.

She married a Tennessee guy named Cory, and they had two daughters, ages eight and ten. I liked him. One little girl was from a previous marriage, and the other was from their own union. They had nice kids, a nice home, and a nice family.

As a kid we always called Jen "the actress." She added drama to things. She was the one to break out the Bible when we were grounded, and she was the one we went to as a substitute mom.

I thought she was doing well, but I soon learned differently. She and Cory had already been divorced and remarried due to infidelities on both sides. Jen was beautiful like a model, and she knew it. She used beauty to work against men to get what she wanted. Having sex with doctors or lawyers was her way of finding a sugar daddy. It was always about her. She also had severe headaches that put her in the emergency room for treatment, where the doctors gave her pills.

Cory, addicted to pills himself, kept his job for years before he was finally fired. I had no idea Jen was taking them too, as a closet pill-head. They both functioned pretty well until night, when they added alcohol to the mix.

I worked miscellaneous jobs such as painting houses, doing roofing, and working at Pizza Hut. Jen worked as a physical therapy aide, helping amputees and others walk.

I was walking to work and looking for something better to do when Jen said, "You should come next door to where I work and look at what they do."

"What's that?"

"They have a lab that makes prosthetics."

I didn't think much about it, but she kept hounding me until one day after work, instead of walking home, I turned in the opposite direction and went to find where Jen worked. It was half a mile down the road. Once I found her, she took me next door.

"I think you can do this," she said. "You know how to use tools."

I looked around in amazement. *I can do this,* I realized.

It was a small town in Tennessee, and my sister was giving me a recommendation, so I thought it would be easy. I was wrong. The man asked about my education.

"You need a bachelor's degree to get a job here," he said.

I was in awe of the place. *No way,* I thought. *Yes way,* I told myself. "Thank you for your time." I left.

I returned to that place every day after work to learn about making legs. The first step was the cast. They took a mold with plaster of Paris bandages until it hardened, then they removed it from the patient to have an exact replica of that person's limb. From there, it went to a sandbox for filling and striping, so someone could modify the mold to make a test socket and check the fit of the weight-bearing part of the limb to ensure comfort. There shouldn't be any pain to the residual limb. Other steps happened after that, but it all began with the sandbox.

I checked in with them daily. The boss always said no until they were backed up with orders.

"You're losing money because the casts in the sandbox are staying in there too long," I pointed out.

He went back into the lab and saw all the casts backing up and agreed. I began filling and stripping casts. I watched people do their own jobs and learned to do all of them quickly, then I offered to help them. They agreed and let me do their jobs too.

The boss came in and saw all his highly paid employees standing around while I did the work of five people. Peter let them go and allowed me to pursue my knowledge through seminars, which taught me different technologies, applications, and fabrication skills. I was a one-man machine, and he knew it. I had no life, just time with my sister, so I was willing to work evenings, weekends, or anything he needed to get the job done in time.

He became and still is my mentor. He was awesome to

allow me to work without having the skills, and he taught me a trade for life that will help people. He was born in Memphis to wonderful, well-off parents. His sister was born with polio and was on a book cover with Elvis Presley, and was also a polio poster child. She was older than Peter and often beat him up with her crutches. She went through life very well, dancing, going to school, and getting on the board of directors for the American Academy for Orthotics and Prosthetics.

Peter told me stories of the slaves who worked around his house when he was a child, and I told him about my past. We became good friends. I helped him do his books–something he wasn't very good at–which taught me what to do and also what not to do.

I moved out of Jen's place, and Cory helped me buy a car. It was a little red Chevy, used but mine, perfect for what I needed.

I continued working days and some weekends, learning to fabricate legs and braces. Peter let Ryan come to work after he returned from the Iraq War, and he did most of the orthotics while I did prosthetics. We got along great. I taught him Peter's way.

I met a patient my age who was a patient of Peter's. He'd lost a leg in a car accident while he was drinking and driving. An outgoing person before the accident, he became a recluse, but I always talked to him and did the work he needed when it came in.

Once, he came in while Peter was on a hospital call. I was the only one there. He had the hardest time telling me he wanted a butt. The socket design on an above-knee patient requires the trim lines to come up high into the groin and buttock area. The plastic edge stuck out of his pants. He wanted something that blended in more with his jeans. He had a fantastic walk, too–not a limp. With his perfect gait and baggie jeans, no one could see his butt.

I took some foam and shaped a butt for him to make him happy. The only thing Jeff did outside the house was learn to golf. He enjoyed it and became good at it. In the meantime, his personality diminished, and it became more difficult to make him smile.

I started reading Peter's magazine called *Amputee Golf,* which had pictures of many amputees golfing. I noticed a tournament in Alabama, which wasn't that far.

I went to Peter and asked, "Is there any way we can help Jeff? I feel he might commit suicide. He's depressed and getting worse."

Peter agreed and gave me his credit card and car keys. Jeff and I drove to Alabama to enter him in the tournament. It was awesome for both of us to see all those courageous people having fun together. They had incredible camaraderie. Jeff was in awe seeing so many people in shorts, showing off their prosthetic arms or legs or both. He kept asking me what the various people had.

I fought back tears and said, "They're just like you, Jeff. Look at them getting around, just like you. They aren't depressed. They're having fun, seeing people and playing golf."

"That's really great."

Jeff went home and eventually married a girl from church he met. He moved out of his parents' house too.

I started attending as many tournaments as I could and became good friends with many of the people I met, including Willie, a man about six feet, five inches tall, who lost his leg at the pelvis. The operation is called a hemipelvectomy, a serious amputation that usually occurs after cancer.

Willie got out there and smacked that ball as hard as everyone else. I made sure I played ahead of him and got people off the green when Willie was driving. He could drive the green. He was and still is amazing, as were many other inspiring people.

We met Mike, who made quite an impression. He was a bilateral above-knee amputee who had his legs blown off by a land mine in Vietnam. He wore red, white, and blue shirts with stars on them every day. He had a custom trailer attached to the back of his golf cart to pull him along. He also had custom forearm crutches made to help get him out of his chair and go to the tee box, where he smacked the ball with custom clubs made just for him. He was good, too!

Another one was Keith, who'd been hit by a train and lost half his body, losing one arm and a leg above the knee. He wore an artificial leg and used only one arm to hit the ball, but he sure hit it hard. We had a blast for those days, playing and meeting everyone. I stayed in touch with those amputees for the next twenty years.

Later in life, I became the state sponsor for several years, hosting those amputees and welcoming them to the Sunshine State to play golf.

When Jeff and I returned from our trip to Alabama, Peter was very glad he let us go. Together, we saved Jeff.

Peter allowed me to continue learning whenever an opportunity presented itself. I lived in fear of abandonment and suppressed my pain for years by working. Helping people at work helped me dissolve my anger, as the patients loved me for what

I did. The appreciation I received and the love I was missing came from the gratitude and satisfaction of my patients.

Once, one of them said, "JoAnn, you have a condo in heaven with your name on it."

Work was easy for me. I was always a loyal person. I was happy to work each day and learn new things.

I saved my money and eventually got in touch with Marcie again. When I visited her in Florida, she said she knew where Mom was and wanted to visit her.

"No way," I said.

"She would love for us to be a family again. We have to try."

I didn't want to go, but I finally gave in.

We visited Mom's trailer, which didn't have room enough for one, let alone five people. Marcie knocked on the door, but no one answered. She knew they were inside because a car was parked there.

"Let's stay until someone comes," she said. "Someone has to come, right?"

We waited until they came out of the trailer. They walked straight to the car like we weren't there. That really hurt.

"I won't leave until they come back," I declared. "It's their home. They have to come back sometime."

Sure enough, they came back and walked to the house, though Brad stopped in front of us.

I cursed him from head to toe. When we were kids, we weren't allowed to talk back, let alone swear. I told him exactly what I thought of him, about how he brainwashed Mom into hating and abandoning her own children. I screamed and hollered for at least ten minutes.

At the end, he asked, "Are you done yet?" He walked into the trailer and got Mom and the other kids. "If you can let it go, we can have a relationship. That is, if you want to see your mom."

I'd wanted to see her because it had been eight years, and if I passed my brothers or sisters on the street, I wouldn't have recognized them. That was another thing that angered me.

They came out, and I hugged each one and cried. I agreed not to talk about the past and instead look to the future. That was a big problem with the older kids–Tom, Jen, and John. They couldn't forgive and constantly asked why they'd been treated so badly.

That visit was when I learned of Marcie and Brad's relationship. It was very awkward. There was a lot of drinking, but many topics couldn't be brought up. If Tom, Jen, and John brought up those subjects when they were drinking, Brad kicked them out until they finally stopped visiting.

A couple years after I moved to Tennessee, Mom got lung cancer. I visited her two times a year on my vacations. Each year, I tried to refrain from bringing up the past and tried to build a relationship with her, but it was hopeless. She didn't want one with me. All she wanted was liquor, beer, and cigarettes. She still didn't care about me. She never had and never would love us. I kept trying for those last few years, kidding myself until the day might come when she said, "I love you," or "I'm proud of you." That would have been great, considering I was making a difference in people's lives each day.

It never happened. Instead, we sat alone one day near her death, and I saw she was scared. I stared at her with all the love a kid could offer her mom.

She looked at me and said, "Quit staring at me!"

That did it. I was livid. "That's it?"

"Yep. That's it."

She never said she was sorry or that she loved me. It was the right time and place to come to terms and be at peace, but she died instead.

I went back to Tennessee. Later, no one told me to come to Florida when Mom was dying in the hospital. I got a call from Jen at two o'clock one morning to tell me Mom was dead and to prepare to drive to Florida the next day.

I cried myself to sleep.

I woke in the morning, wondering if it was a dream, when I heard a knock at the door. It was Jen.

"Let's go to Florida," she said.

It was real. I packed, and we drove down.

The funeral was one of the most bizarre things I've ever seen. Mom's family came, or some of them at least, the day before to gather at Brad's. Neighbors brought food. I'd never been to a funeral before. We didn't go to Aunt Sara's funeral when she died at thirty-two.

I was really distraught. The relatives spoke only to them-selves, pointing and talking about us.

The next day was worse. Everyone gathered in the funeral home, where the body was in a casket. A man performed a small service, then we had to go down the road for the burial.

We walked outside to the parking lot, and the mood was terrible. People drank toasts from their trucks, calling it an Irish wake. Meanwhile, tempers flared between Tom and me because they weren't taking Mom's body anywhere. They were partying.

A man said Mom wasn't going anywhere but to a freezer until Brad paid the bill he owed. Brad hadn't told anyone.

When I asked Brad, he said he had no money. I was in shock. Mom was going into a freezer, and no one seemed to care. She treated me like crap for my entire life, but still–a freezer? I couldn't do it.

Liza said she'd loan me the money to finish the burial and pay for the service. The man wanted $5,000, so Liza went to the bank and got the money.

We finished the service and went back to Brad's. I didn't know how funerals were supposed to work, but I doubted they were done like that.

The next day, a friend of Mom's came by. He looked like someone who never had a dime. He came to hang out with Mom and Brad and sometimes slept outside on the ground. To my surprise, he gave me $5,000.

"It's what I want to do," he said.

"Thank you," I told him. When I repaid Liza, I said, "Thank you. I owe you one."

Later in life, I made her mother a free polio leg brace.

Soon after I returned to Tennessee, I realized how much I missed Florida and the fishing. I tried fishing lakes in Tennessee, but I never caught anything, not even a catfish.

I realized that we only lived once, so we should be happy in life. Mom died at fifty-two. Her sister died at forty-six. Another sister died at thirty-two and my father passed at fifty-nine. Was it in my genes that I'd die young too? I hoped not, but I knew I'd better have fun while I could.

I told Peter my thoughts about leaving Tennessee, and he promised to give me a good recommendation. Of course, he wanted me to stay. I sent résumés to different companies, including one near Brad and the kids. I guess I did that because I had no one and wanted to be loved by someone.

It didn't happen, though. I took the Tampa job and worked for two years before going to Sarasota for another year. I saved money living in a single-bedroom apartment with my German Shepherd while I saved a down payment for a home. I passed my exam to be a licensed, certified orthotist and continued studying prosthetics. I got it because of my experience, without a college degree. I felt proud of myself.

Brad and the kids continued to abuse me, asking for money because I had a job, and they didn't. Maria and Sonny lived next door to them. She had two kids and didn't work, but she still somehow took care of their bills and our parents' bills for years. I never knew how she did it. Cole bought a truck for work, but he refused to go.

I got an opportunity to start my own business in 2008 with a partner. I was twenty-nine and I jumped at the chance, realizing I could do it. Tim was more competent than me.

The business started out well, just as planned. He loved

fishing like I did, so we got along very well. We fished a lot after work on the shoreline, trying for snook off the rocks. It was a blast, and he was a great fisherman, born in Florida, so he knew all the ropes about inshore fishing. I still love him today. He was a good man who taught me a lot more than fishing. He was the best orthotist I ever met. He taught me to take a mold of a patient's back, then lay the X-ray on the mold of the patient and bend the metal to accommodate or correct scoliosis of the spine. That was a special technique that few people knew how to do.

He also taught me how to go to Tampa General Hospital to install HALO on cervical injury patients in ICU. We got their weight, height, and had a formula to set the torque wrench for drilling screws into the skull to hold the brace in place and allow the cervical area to heal in proper alignment. The head and neck were kept immobile while the patient was healing. We replaced the chest pads to the HALO because after a while they stank, because the patient couldn't shower. We came in every four weeks to do that. It was an intense job because we had to move the head to replace the chest plate. It was a nerve-wracking job; one wrong move might paralyze the patient. We did that for two years at that hospital and others nearby. After that experience, I felt confident I could do it alone at any time.

Everything went well until Tim decided, after one year, he'd rather play golf. I came to work one day and saw the checkbook had a check signed out, and the stocks had been signed over to me. Tim took half the money and left! I freaked out and started crying. I called him, begging him to come back.

He refused, and I worked long days and nights. I had an

opportunity to make a prosthetic leg for Mrs. DuPont, the heir to DuPont plastics. She was very grateful. I made a leg for Mrs. Hood from Hood milk. I made one for Mr. Mote from the Mote Aquarium. He was a very funny man. I got to make a leg brace for a giraffe in Busch Gardens. That was really cool. Her name was Callie, and she was born premature. Her two front legs buckled, which made her fall often. The keepers planned to kill her, so we took casts of her legs and made custom leg braces for her. They fit perfectly, and suddenly, she could stand, walk, and not die.

We also made a leg brace for an ostrich, an artificial leg for a red-tailed hawk, and many dog legs and braces. We even made one for a horse. I volunteered for all of those projects, refusing any pay, and the patients were extremely grateful. I just wanted to give back and help others with my abilities.

I kept a photo album of those times. When the hawk had trouble with its leg, I was called back out and found it had a sore on the stump. I needed a stump sock, but the leg was so small, I couldn't sew or buy one. I needed something special.

I went to Walmart and bought Barbie doll socks. When we put them on the hawk, they worked great. The newspaper ran an article on that one. The keepers planned to release the bird to the wild, but I suggested they use it for research with children just in case the leg came off, and the hawk couldn't defend himself. That worked out really well.

The same thing happened with the ostrich. It needed to flock, and the owners asked me to come to the farm to see if it would flock with other small ostriches. That farm was unreal. Everything had to be just right, even the temperature of the drinking water.

On my day off, I drove to Myakka to the farm. Everything went well with the other birds, so the owners asked if I'd look at the mama bird's bad eye. Ostriches were very expensive animals, and I began to feel like a vet. I agreed to take a look. They took me around a corner to the mother and father ostriches, and they were humongous!

"The lower two feet of the fence are left open deliberately so you can roll out if you need to," the man told me. "They can kill a lion with one kick. They can kick forward too. They can run at forty-five miles an hour."

If they thought I'd get in the pen with those things, they were mistaken. I assessed the situation and said I'd return in a day with a solution. "Don't feed her. I want her hungry when I get back."

I went to Walmart and bought a squirt gun with my own money. I never charged for cases like this. I put eye drops into the squirt gun and got a carrot.

The next day, the female ostrich came right up to me for her meal, and I squirted her in the eye. The people were amazed.

"Y'all didn't think I'd get in the pen with them, did you?" I asked.

The eye healed, and the ostrich was saved. A pair of ostriches cost $10,000 due to their extremely lean meat, which people loved.

The next case was a dwarf cow that was only three feet high at full growth. She had a bad front leg. She took a few steps, then the leg buckled, and her face hit the ground. It was very sad. I went to assess the situation. The owners lived on a farm in Dade City near the Bellamy Brothers. All of her animals were rescues, and none were to be eaten. They would live long lives. I told them not to feed the cow before I arrived.

I held out a sugar cube, and the cow came right up to me. Once I saw what was needed, I took a cast of the cow's leg and left.

When I returned with the finished brace, I added it to her leg with a sock for an interface, then I used Velcro to keep it shut. The cow was able to walk without falling over, and the woman was amazed and grateful.

A TV crew was there, and they filmed the whole thing. When I drove off, they focused on my truck going down the driveway with my vanity plate, LEGMAKR.

While I was sponsoring the Florida amputee golf tournament, I met a woman who lost her arm below the elbow. I asked why she wasn't wearing her prosthesis.

"No one can make one that's comfortable for me," she replied.

"I can."

When I gave her the arm, she loved it. She made a hole in one with that arm and was extremely happy and grateful.

I also started a weekly amputee support group for amputees to meet and get to know each other. Another motto of mine was, "See one, do one, teach one." A new amputee would come to the group and see plenty of other amputees walking, talking, and doing everyday things they did before their amputation. It was very inspirational for the newcomers and allowed older amputees to gain friends.

I met a guy I liked who was a lot older and much wiser. He was a good pool player, as was I. He enjoyed fishing as much as I did too, so we got along well.

I eventually found a home on a canal with a pool, just like I wanted. It needed work, but I could do that. The yard was fenced for my dog, which was perfect. I bought an eighteen-foot Ranger boat and learned to fish the flats. Eventually, I bought a twenty-two-foot bay boat.

We became serious enough that we moved in together. I bought a time share on Captiva Island, where we fished and golfed for a whole week. It was fun catching snook, redfish, and trout.

I thought offshore fishing might be fun, so I started chartering boats to learn more. We went to Golden Marina and bought a twenty-nine-foot MAKO boat. We learned a lot from Carl Golden and his friend, Anthony Manali, at Perico, where they had fishing seminars we attended. Anthony showed people how to throw his net for bait.

We started fishing in the bay and worked our way offshore, learning about radar and electronics. We rarely caught anything, but it was fun trying, sort of like hunting in the sea. I just enjoyed being on the water.

I eventually grew out of the MAKO and bought a thirty-two-foot Hydra-Sports boat with triple engines to go offshore. We hired Anthony Manali to teach us some offshore tricks. I learned a lot from him and we caught plenty of fish, which was fun.

Rob ran the computer center of Tampa General Hospital and had a wealth of knowledge. I was lousy with computers, and he taught me a lot. He also helped at night making legs and braces. He finally quit the hospital and worked with me full time. He started at the bottom like I did, but I eventually had him certified. When I told Brad I'd like him to meet Rob, he refused. I really didn't want Rob to meet my crazy family, anyway. Rob didn't want to meet them either. We stayed away and lived our lives.

Marcie came to visit with her boyfriend, one of many. She had two kids, but they didn't live with her, and I thanked God for that. Instead, they lived with their grandmother.

Marcie liked crack cocaine and meth. Tom would take anything he could get. John's drug was heroin, Jen's was pills, Cole's was meth, and Carmine would also take anything. None of them were willing to stop. John died eventually, but the rest are still addicts.

Marcie arrived at 11:30 p.m. one night with her boyfriend and a case of beer. Rob woke me to say they were at the door.

"What?" I asked. "What time is it?"

Furious, I went to the door, wondering what they thought they were doing at such an hour when I had to work in the morning.

"I'm calling the cops," I told them. "I'm sure they're looking for you for something."

She immediately turned around and got into her truck. Then I saw Cole was with them. He must've shown her where I lived.

One day sometime later, I stopped in a store for my daily coffee when an old man told me he was Brad's friend. I remembered him and said hello.

"Brad died recently, and it wasn't pretty," he told me.

I didn't think it would be, I thought, *after what he did.*

"He was sixty-one and suffered a long time."

I felt sorry, but I was glad too. I knew Brad's time had come to justify what he did to God, and I knew I wouldn't be seeing him, Mom, or John in heaven when I got there.

I was the only one of Mom's children who went to her grave and took care of it. Sometimes, I filled my truck bed with debris from the grave, taking off the old flowers and putting on new ones.

I heard Brad was cremated, with his ashes placed on top of Mom's grave. That was another reminder that time passed quickly, and I knew I'd better have fun while I could. I knew I'd never have kids, and that was fine. I would have wanted my children to love me, but I was too scared that I'd treat them badly. I would be fine. I was as strong as a lion. I wouldn't marry Rob, either. He wasn't the one for me, and I wondered if there ever would be someone.

Rob and I were together for nine years. Our business went well. We did a lot together, donating time to help amputees, animals, and families. We held annual picnics at Coquina Beach, which was wheelchair accessible. We even held a wedding, and I caught the bouquet. We took amputees on dinner cruises with their families. Rob helped me make the legs for Mrs. DuPont and Mrs. Hood.

We had a lot of fun together and he taught me a lot, but when I caught him cheating the second time, I said, "Pack up and leave."

"I was planning to leave when you were in Inverness. I already started packing."

After he left, I felt very upset. My feelings were hurt. We'd worked hard to make our business succeed, but our personal lives were left out. We both worked at our separate jobs, going separate places each day.

The business grew to include three locations along Florida's west coast. We were lean with employees and good at fabrication, so our turnaround time was quick. Thanks to Rob, we had lots of referrals. Stacie, who worked with Rob every day, said Rob taught her enough to do his job when he left. I trusted her and agreed to have her take over his work. I couldn't possibly do his job or hers. By then, everything was on computers. It was very difficult for me to do my job and office work on top of that.

I was very distraught about Rob's leaving and needed to get past that difficult time. I went to Carl Golden again and bought a boat from him. I could trust his word. He was in a wheelchair for life, and we made a good connection. I also asked for a captain for hire to go fishing with me. Since Carl knew Rob, I told him what happened and how I needed to go fishing to pass the time. He recommended Captain Anthony, a man I once hired with Rob to fish with us and teach us a few things. I kept his name in my phone contacts as Anthony Mullet. I'd heard him called the "mullet man."

I called Captain Anthony and set up a time to meet at the boat one morning. I had to bring the crew, all the gear, and the food.

We met at the dock at the appointed time. I asked Cole, my brother, to come and had to pay him for it, because I didn't know Captain Anthony that well and didn't want him throwing anyone overboard and taking my boat.

We had a blast. We caught more fish than we ever caught in our lives. Captain Anthony was good, and the fun took my mind off Rob. Most captains screamed at their mates, which took the fun out of hiring them. Anthony let us catch fish ourselves. He didn't hook the fish and then give us the rod to reel it in like some captains do. No, he let us set the hook *and* reel it in ourselves. I'd never seen anyone so calm before, yet also filled with so much excitement. It was fun to catch fish, and not just go fishing for them.

Each time we went fishing, we caught more and more fish

and had more and more fun. At the end of the trip, I paid the captain and gave him a generous tip so that he would say yes the next time I asked.

We began fishing in May and went at it hard for three months, every day the weather allowed. Meanwhile, my employees said they could handle the business, so I should go ahead and have fun. I did.

We went offshore fifty or sixty miles–which took a while to get out that far–then we fished and came back. Anthony and I talked a lot. His hobbies included fishing and golfing like mine. His ex-wife cheated on him and broke up their family. That hurt him deeply. I felt the same way about Rob.

After three months of fishing, our friendship blossomed. I was falling for Captain Anthony, and I realized Rob never made me feel that way. In fact, no one ever had. Anthony cared about people so much, it was unreal. What really got me was one day after fishing all day, my brother's car broke down, and he wanted me to drive him home, which was an hour away. After drinking while fishing, I said, "I can't drive."

"I'll give you a ride home," Anthony said, without knowing my brother.

I was astonished and impressed that he'd offer to help someone he didn't know. That was when I began to fall for Anthony. Soon, I realized I'd never been in love before, because I never felt those feelings.

I started chasing Anthony pretty hard, and we had a blast together. He listened to me, we laughed a lot, and we enjoyed each other's company. My life improved every day.

After three months and some lunch dates, I asked Anthony out for a real date, and he agreed. I picked him up in my beautiful yellow Corvette–that I drove only for special occasions–and took him to the Sarasota Ritz Carlton and had them valet the car as we checked in and had our luggage sent up to the presidential suite. We went into the concierge level first, a special area upstairs that required a key for entry. Once we were inside, anything we wanted was available: coffee, tea, snacks, and food all day. If I didn't see something I wanted, all I had to do was ask, and they would provide it.

Anthony ordered his White Russian and gasped at the views. He told me how he fished in certain areas, but he'd never seen them from such a viewpoint. I'd never done anything like that before, but then, I'd never felt like that before either. All those long, fourteen-hour days were paying off.

The room was amazing. It had rose petals from the front foyer to the living room to the bedroom, with a heart on the bed made of rose petals that also led to the bathroom with a hot tub, illuminated by candles everywhere. It was very romantic. We had a kitchen with all the kinds of ice cream anyone could want, a full bar, a dining room that seated ten, and a living room with a wraparound porch overlooking Sarasota Bay.

What a first date! Anthony was unbelievably patient with me. He listened, he cared, and he loved me. I was falling more and more in love with him. All I could think about every day was him.

He had a wonderful family. His parents were precious, and they loved him. His children were nice, and his cousins, aunts, and uncles were wonderful to me. They treated me like family.

We dated for two years, and I wanted to marry him. I asked his parents to come to lunch at the beach where they and Anthony lived. They accepted and met us at the restaurant.

I flew a plane with a banner over the beach that read, "I love you, Anthony. Will you marry me? JoAnn."

He accepted. We had a wonderful wedding and an unbelievable honeymoon. I always thought I'd never get married, but if I did, I would never divorce. We did it right.

Since our first date was at the Ritz Carlton, we decided to get married there. They gave me the presidential suite as a wedding gift since we had the suite for our first date, and I paid for the wedding party to stay as well. I couldn't dance, yet I knew we had to dance at our wedding, so I hired a professional named Geno to teach us. He came to the house for six months until we could do a Foxtrot to the song, "A Wink and a Smile." We looked like pros and gave a good performance.

More than two hundred guests attended the wedding. Anthony's Uncle Joe was a very worldly man, and he said he'd been to some nice weddings, but never one that good. That meant a lot to me. I didn't have a wedding planner, and I took care of all the details myself.

We had the wedding in one hall and the reception in the next one. It was beautiful. I cried, even though I told everyone who warned me I would that I would never cry at my own wedding. The moment I saw Anthony crying, I began to cry, and the whole place was crying after that.

A wonderful harpist played as we walked down the aisle, and she played later with her band. She was very talented. We had her back to play for our first anniversary too.

We had a special crab cake for Anthony and another for us. The food was top quality. One of the best parts was that Maria attended. Despite not feeling well because of dental issues and her constant battle with diabetes, she told me how beautiful the day was. That was the best day I ever had.

I always wanted to go to Hawaii so I said if I ever got married, I'd go there on my honeymoon, and Anthony agreed.

I booked us two first-class tickets for one week in Maui and one week in Honolulu. I met Usher on the plane out there and got his autograph.

We had a stretch limo pick us up to take us to the Maui Ritz Carlton, because the Ritz name was significant for us. Our suite overlooked the West Maui Mountains.

We played golf at the Kapalua PGA course and rode horseback in the pineapple fields overlooking the Pacific Ocean. The beauty was astonishing. We never played on a better golf course in our lives. We made great memories we would always remember.

After one week, we caught a flight to Honolulu to get a small limo to bring us to our next location. When we arrived at the Hilton, I noticed the place was small and mentioned that to Anthony. We found cobwebs in the windows, and the glass was dirty. I was a clean freak and noticed things like that.

We checked in and got our room. It turned out to be just a regular room. I left Anthony when he took a nap and ate some chocolates, then I went down to the desk to ask if there was a mistake with our room. The receptionist said there wasn't.

"Do you have a better room? I'm on my honeymoon."

"There are none available."

I went into the lounge and put a $100 bill on the bar when I asked for a beer. The bartender returned with my beer.

"Can I ask a question?"

"No problem. What can I do for you?"

"I'm on my honeymoon, but all I have is a regular room.

I checked at the front desk and didn't have any luck. Am I at the right hotel?"

"You're at the wrong place. You want the Halekulani Hotel. You'd like it there."

I left the money on the bar. "Thank you." I carried my beer to the front desk and asked to see the manager, then I sat down and waited.

A woman came out with another woman behind her.

"She's in training," the first woman told me. "How can I help you?"

"I'm on my honeymoon, but all I have is a regular room. I asked for an upgrade but was told there's nothing available. How is the Halekulani? I'm thinking about moving over there."

"They've got nothing on us," the first woman said.

Behind her, the second woman shook her head.

"I think I might be in the wrong hotel."

The woman behind her nodded.

"Have them call me," I told the manager. "I'll be in my room."

A minute after I got to my room, the manager of the Halekulani called. "How can I help you?"

"I'm on my honeymoon. Do you have anything available?"

"We have the Vera Wang suite available. It's just what you're looking for."

"I'll take it."

He sent a stretch limo to pick us up. When we arrived, the manager and two butlers, Ray and Francis, greeted us with fresh Hawaiian leis to place around our necks. We were treated like royalty.

They escorted us to our room and told us that Kid Rock and Gwen Stefani had been in recently.

"Gwen sang a song for me," Ray added, "because I couldn't go into town for her concert."

We stayed there for a week overlooking Diamond Head on Waikiki Beach. We went on a submarine to the reef. We couldn't go in the water because there was an outbreak of box jellyfish. The news showed people running from the water in pain.

We met Naomi, Anthony's sister, who gave us a tour of the island. We were in love, and everything got better each day we were together.

This is when Anthony told me he was sitting upstairs one day, lonely and depressed, when an angel told him not to worry, and that he was going to meet a girl named JoAnn. He had thought, *I don't even know a JoAnn.*

W e've been together for fourteen years. I love him and his wonderful family tremendously. I chased him pretty hard because of my love for him.

I stepped away from my business, retiring after eighteen years in business for myself, with twenty-five years of service in the industry. "When one door closes, another opens," the Lord said.

I did a lot of fishing. Anthony is on his fiftieth season and needed my help. We went fishing with Mr. Almer, the CEO of a car company. He flew us down in his private jet, which had two pilots and a stewardess named Victoria, who laid out a fine spread, including Dom Pérignon champagne. We flew to Key West to enter the world sailfish tournament with Joe Almer.

We were picked up in a Hummer limo and went to his boat, a seventy-four-foot Viking, a top-of-the-line craft. There we met General Norman Schwartzkopf, Kelly Clarkson, and IGFA's Guy Harvey. I became a six-time world record holder for catching fish. Who else can say that? Jim knew that between Anthony's three world records and my six, we would be of good help to the crew. Anthony is a legend on the island of Anna Maria and has been fishing professionally his whole life. He has his techniques to find the fish, and he knows how to rig the tackle for world records.

The day I set my first world record, it was my birthday and we were just dating still and he was trying to impress me. He told me we were going fishing for my birthday, and I laughed since fishing was something I did practically every day at this point. He said to me, "But today for your birthday you are going to catch a world-record fish."

Sure enough, we headed offshore and we loaded the boat with all the gear and he added a little rod and reel. I asked, "What are you going to do with that little thing?"

He said, "You are going to catch a world record on it." He stopped shorter than where we normally stopped and also kept different baits than we normally kept. He said, "Okay JoAnn, grab that little rod and get your world record so we can go fishing."

I attached the selected bait to my hook as instructed and sent it down, with everyone watching. I completely ran out of line and knew I couldn't fish like that, so I immediately turned the reel three full turns, and there came an eight-pound mangrove snapper! He pulled drag but I knew I didn't have much, so I cupped my reel then let it go, then cupped it again until I got that fish out of the water and into the boat. Once Anthony saw the size of that fish, he immediately congratulated me on my new world record!

My other record-winning fish include a sixty-pound black grouper, red groupers, and a few mangrove snappers. I also have an all-tackle world record for the biggest fish ever caught by a man or woman on any line class. The fish that won me that record was an oceanic puffer fish.

Going to Alaska was our all-time favorite trip; we spent the entire time fishing for halibut and king salmon. We took Anthony's best man and his wife with us since they could never afford to go to Alaska. We went to a hatchery for salmon and learned all about them, and also went to a glacier and learned about global warming. We even ziplined.

One of our captains during a trip to Alaska taught me that if you cut the salmon open and take out the roe, you can put the roe on a hook and use it as bait. It's like candy that the halibut can't resist. After hearing that handy tip, I asked the captain how big of a halibut he thought I'd catch that day. I pulled out a wad of money and said, "You get a dollar tip for every pound of fish you catch today. Am I going to catch an eighty pounder or a three-hundred-pounder?" He agreed to my bargain. That day, I caught a 301-pound halibut and gave him a $301 tip. He was very pleased I kept my word and has since come to Florida and fished with us.

We opened a little fish shack on the beach where we live and sold the fish we caught in order to pay our bills. That worked well because we loved fishing. We met Skip Holtz, Lou Holtz, Joey Galloway, and Tony Dungy, along with many others. Tony Dungy let us put on his Super Bowl ring and take photos with it. Another time, he autographed his book, *Quiet Strength*, and told me he loses fish in the rocks too.

Joey Galloway expects "Anthony's famous fish dip" whenever he comes to fish. We flew over the Bahamas on a private jet and fished for mahi-mahi. I almost caught a fish so large it would have won me another world record, but it broke off.

I could never get enough of going crabbing with Anthony. It's so much fun. We catch blue and stone crabs, which are very tasty. Another thing he does with me is he takes me into the pass to fish for big grouper in shallow water; grouper are very aggressive fighters.

Anthony was eventually offered a deal from Mrs. Golden to buy her home on the island. I didn't need a house because I had one at Apollo Beach, but since I paid it off, I thought another house would be a good investment. I bought it, fixed it up, and paid it off. It's a beautiful waterfront home.

Carl Golden owned a Viking dealership on the island and asked us to fish with him occasionally. We caught blue marlin on the oil rigs in the middle of the Gulf of Mexico, just off Louisiana. We caught yellowfin tuna too, including a big one.

Even after hearing all my crazy stories, Anthony still loves me. That is true love. He inspired me to write this book because he couldn't believe I survived my early life. It wasn't easy, but I refused to give up like my siblings did.

Looking back, I can't believe I lived through it all. I hope my story inspires other children. If I can make it, so can they.

My wonderful husband has more than two hundred fishing nets and taught me to throw a net. During the summer months, one of my all-time favorite things is to catch Spanish mackerel off the beach. We have a wagon we load up with an ice chest, nets, rods, tackle, bait holder, and more, and we wheel it from the house to the beach and get in the water, catching bait with the net and putting it on a floating holder. I usually bring two or three rods in the wagon.

One day, I was fishing in the Gulf alone, catching more Spanish mackerels when a little girl approached me.

"What are you doing on our island?" I asked.

"I'm here with my foster family."

"How do you like them?"

"I like them. They're looking for a family that will love me. My daddy did bad things to me."

"Would you like to fish with me?"

"Yes."

She got my spare rod from the wagon, and we caught Spanish mackerel together. As we walked from the water, I said, "I was in a foster care program when I was a kid. I understand what you went through."

She looked at me in awe.

I wrapped my arm around her. "You know what? You're going to be okay."

ABOUT THE AUTHOR

JoAnn Manali lives in Anna Maria Island, Florida, and spends as much time as possible fishing with her true love, Anthony, in the Gulf of Mexico. She is a six-time IGFA World Record holder for various fish species. She loves to play golf, cook, and watch sunsets on the beach. She has a huge abundance of friends from all over the country, as well as the world, because of her and Anthony's reputation of supplying quality fishing and fish products at Capt Anthony's Seafood Market in Anna Maria.